Eternal Life Begins
at Salvation

by D. Michael Cotten

ISBN# 978-1-936497-25-6

Contact the Author at
dmichaelcotten@att.net

Searchlight Press
Who are you looking for?
Publishers of thoughtful Christian books since 1994.
5634 Ledgestone Drive
Dallas, Texas 75214
888.896.6081
info@Searchlight-Press.com
www.Searchlight-Press.com

Dedication

To everyone who receives a word from the Lord and struggles with their ability to accomplish the task, we must remember who opened the Red Sea, gave strength to Moses and Aaron, and raised Jesus from the dead. It is GOD who will accomplish His Goal through us using His Power.

Table of Contents

Notes

INTRODUCTION

GOD is eternal
GOD's realm is the only realm that is eternal
GOD made mankind in his Image
and part of mankind is eternal.

When we believe that GOD is the Creator of the world, and that his awesome grandeur, intelligence, beauty, power, enveloped in perfectness is our inadequate attempt to describe GOD. Then we must become enlightened with being made in the image of GOD? Who is this GOD that would design and create this world for Mankind and Mankind for GOD? Mankind is not an accident; we are a creation and therefore have a concept of destiny and purpose. We have self-esteem, self-concept, and an awareness of a moral and ethical standard because we are the product of creation. Having been made in the Image of Almighty GOD, mankind wants to know its creator and its purpose.

You used to be dead because of your sins and acts of disobedience.
You walked in the ways of the Natural world and
obeyed the Ruler of the Powers of the Air,
who is still at work among the disobedient.
Indeed, we all once lived this way —
we followed the passions of our old nature and
obeyed the wishes of our old nature
and our own thoughts.
In our natural condition we were headed for God's wrath, just like everyone else.

But God is so rich in mercy and loves us with such intense love that,
even when we were dead because of our acts of disobedience,
he brought us to life along with Jesus, the Messiah —
it is by grace that you have been delivered.

Eternal Life Begins at Salvation, 5

That is, God raised us up with Jesus, the Messiah, and seated us with him in heaven, in order to exhibit in the ages to come how infinitely rich is his grace, how great is his kindness toward us who are united with Jesus, the Messiah,

For you have been delivered by grace through trusting, and even this is not your accomplishment but God's gift.

You were not delivered by your own actions;
    therefore no one should boast.
            For we are of God's making,
                created in union with Jesus, the Messiah,
                    for a life of good actions
                already prepared by God for us to do.
                    Ephesians 2:1-8

Only the GOD that created all things
    would sacrifice part of Himself
        to offer eternal life to believers
            who choose right standing with GOD.

We are not human beings having a Spiritual experience.
We are Spiritual beings having a human experience.
Our view of GOD determines what we think of ourselves.

Chapter 1

Created and Designed by GOD

Einstein is credited with saying, "**You would have to be an idiot to look at this creation and not know there is a Creator**", the closest Einstein quote I can find is similar "In the view of such harmony in the cosmos which I, with my limited human mind, am able to recognize**, there are yet people** who say, there is no God". Either comment confirms the same result of stupidity for those who don't believe in a Creator GOD.

Think about the enormity of this statement by Einstein, one of the smartest men that ever lived, who worked in the unseen world of atomic power. Atoms, etc. moving at incredible speed inside objects that are stationary. In Einstein's opinion, there is no planet in the world like our planet because GOD made or remodeled our planet. THE OTHER BILLION STARS AND PLANETS DO NOT HAVE THE ABILITY TO SUSTAIN HUMAN, ANIMAL, or PLANT LIFE. None of the other planets have water, or oxygen based atmospheres suitable for life. The other planets would not have light except for the lights **GOD made for us**. Do you ever take time to contemplate the incredible world in which we live? Have you considered what it took for GOD to make this blob into a planet that can sustain Human life, plant life, and animal life? None of the other stars and planets can sustain life of any kind, nor do we see any of the mineral structures of a plant growing planet. GOD made life and without Him there is no life, at all. What is the chance, that without GOD, our planet is the only planet or star that can sustain life out of the billions of stars and planets that we can see? That should tell you how special "we are to GOD". Notice I did not say, our GOD is special to us, it is the love of GOD toward us that makes our planet special and GOD's gift of

His Son seals that love of God for us. GOD made the world and then made mankind and gave us the world and everything in it.

The scientific proof of DNA or gene sequencing has virtually closed the book on the" Theory of Evolution" although its proponents are not going away for the saddest of reasons. Recently in reading Dr. James Merritt's great book "GOD, I've got a question" He quotes 1967 Nobel Peace prize recipient for Physiology and a former professor of Biology at Harvard University, who said,

> "There are only two possibilities as to how life arose; one is spontaneous generation to evolution, the other is supernatural creative act of GOD. There is no third possibility…the belief that life comes from non-living matter, was scientifically disproved one hundred and twenty years ago by Louis Pasteur and others, that leaves us with only one possibility…that life arose from a creative act of GOD. **But I will not accept that Philosophy because I don't want to believe in GOD**, therefore I choose to believe in that which I know is scientifically impossible, spontaneous generation leading to evolution."

It is very sad to see a smart man like Dr. George Wald choose to believe in something he understands is false. The Bible warned us about men like this man. He desperately needs our prayers that he might see the light. Dr. Martin Luther King said, 'There is nothing more dangerous than "Sincere ignorance" or "Conscientious stupidity".'

Also, there was another Harvard Professor quoted, Dr. Lewontin, who said "even **while admitting the "patent absurdity" of much evolutionary theory"** said simply,

> "We cannot allow a divine foot in the door."

Again Einstein said it best. "You would have to be **an idiot** to look at this creation and **not know** there was a creator". What keeps smart men like this from wanting to have a relationship with the creator of the world, and can you think of one advantage to their life, that a world without GOD would give them?

A believer's view of GOD is the basis for what we think of ourselves, for example, if you do not believe in creation by GOD, then life itself has no meaning because there is no purpose, no end game, and no life after death for cosmic accidents. Existing will be what you make of it within the framework of the society, if there is a society. But if this "devil may care" way of living is subject to the Creator GOD's meaning, for our lives, then there may be "Hell to pay" pardon the pun, but it was so appropriate.

On February 4, 2014 a two hour debate Creation versus evolution between Bill Nye, the Science Guy, and Ken Ham of the Creation Museum, the evolution side came down to the breaking point over dating the oldest fossils, but the dating systems were all designed by man. The ice rings test, carbon dating, atomic change and many more dating methods all came to the conclusion that the earth was millions of years old, but the evolution side could not show one good example of evolution now or in history and could not explain man and his attributes. The evolution side could not offer **any explanations** or proofs of the faculties of mankind or the dilemma for evolutionists that each specie has a male and a female. What are the chances of a cosmic accident producing man and then a woman, and male and female in all animals, not to mention plants? There is no consistency in the argument that the first being was a cosmic accident. Where did the females come from and how did they get here and why would all things with life have a male and female in plants, animals, and humans?

The difference between a created person and cosmic accidents, among others, is that a GOD created person has a mind, will, and emotions and a soul. A soul is an important part of a person and not part of an accident. GOD has a mind, will, and emotions and he installed one in all humans. Matthew 12:18 Acts 16:6 Ephesians 4:25-32 Self-esteem, self-concept, awareness of a moral and ethical standard, a sense of destiny, origin and purpose comes from our concept of Creation by GOD. A cosmic accident producing life cannot give you anything from which to base your existence. Animal and human offspring are prisoners of their minds and must be taught to be free. Without knowledge the Humans will be enslaved to its primary needs of the body, if they are to exist.

It takes more faith to believe evolution than Creation. Even if you could convince yourself that evolution is real and that something living came from things that never lived, your existence would have no purpose. Hope has a destiny and you cannot have destiny without a Creator. Destiny has by definition a future. **If you are a cosmic accident and your view of GOD is; there is no god**, the result will be there is no future and no value for life. Society crumbles because the lack of respect for life and expands to: disrespect for law, property, marriage, or the pursuit of happiness. The world of the cosmic accident producing a life-form that starts as a tadpole or any other small celled creature has no reason to evolve as a man, woman, animal, plant or tree. Accidental spontaneous generation to life is an unbelievable premise and doesn't speak to the millions of species of plants, trees, animal, and insects.

Countries and human beings, that base their existence on a godless society, are destined to have no hope. Examine present day existence in China to see a disregard for life "up close and personal". For decades, Chinese families have been restricted to one child and because these families thought a male child could help bring in more income to support the family; many female children were killed at birth or aborted. The consequence to this disregard for female life is now there are very few women for the men to marry and millions of babies murdered. **Your view of yourself, if there is no GOD,** will be full of fear; fear of losing life, limb, property, children, or being subjected to slavery of the strongest. Existing is living without a purpose for life and there cannot be purpose to existing without GOD.

Atheist, evolutionists, and secularists want to live in countries where the country was founded on GOD and His instructions, and where the laws allow freedom. The atheist etc. complain about the laws that give them freedom and the irony is the laws were based on "in GOD we Trust". Make a note, there are no immigration quotas restricting relocation to countries who don't respect life. Generally, there is a line to get out of Nations that don't respect life and in fact, many countries who don't respect life will not allow anyone to leave.

Atheists might argue, **why won't our existence be just like America, but without GOD**? The answer is; the goals of a country, nation, gang, or tribe developed **without respect for GOD created life**, will be based on the control of the strongest group or individual. Even in America, gangs, bullies, vigilantes, and drug cartels all operate on a society or internal government controlled by the strongest or the meanest. The only motive for action in a gang or cartel is self-preservation. Most countries, **without** a foundation based on GOD, have or had tribal leaders or Kings who thought they were god or made their own gods or worshiped objects such as the sun or the stars. **In a country, where GOD is given credit for creating life**, the attitude toward individual liberties for that created life, lead to laws and cultural norms that are centered on protecting personal freedoms.

Can you name a country or society started by Atheists or evolutionists?

Can you name a godless society in which you want to be a significant part or even visit? How did any godless society get its governmental structure if it has one?

Can you think of a godless society that respects women?
> When atheist hears about ethnic cleansing, they probably thank GOD they live in America, if they lived in a Muslim country they would be killed with the Christians without Heaven as their prize.

In a Godless society, if you are not the strongest and meanest, you will be poor, and many times your hope will be death. All the great nations with freedoms for the people, were founded on GOD. **Only GOD can offer hope because the future is in his hand.** The atheist believes that existing itself is their only purpose and death is the end.

**Your own body will convince you
GOD is The Creator.**

Who do you think designed your bodies functioning systems?
From the time you are conceived and are just large enough to be seen with a magnifying glass . . . **60 trillion cells, 100 thousand miles** of nerve fiber, **60 thousand miles** of vessels carrying blood around the body, **250 bones**, to say nothing of joints, ligaments and muscles will grow in to your body. Your eyes are driven by converting 130 million light sensitive receptor impulses to a photochemical reaction that transforms light into electrical impulses that go to the brain to produce pictures in your brain of what you are seeing. **The chances you are <u>not</u> designed by GOD but evolved from anything**; is the same odds as a tornado blowing through your town and leaving a new 18 hole championship golf course ready to play the US Open Championship. Can you imagine anything short of a creative act of GOD that could make your body, soul, and spirit?

Psalm 139:14 I will praise thee; for I am fearfully and wonderfully made: marvelous are thy works; and that my soul knoweth right well.

While Mankind's bodies may be the most intricate of GOD's creations, the material parts of our world are complex and show the artistry of the building blocks GOD designed to work together to produce our worlds. The power inherent in the atoms, molecules, Ions, and other building blocks that GOD designed to run our worlds are involved in every aspect of our life. Every aspect is a scientific mystery and generally we have no idea how it works. Every morning, as you wake and move your little toe, or open your eyes, or hear the rain, you can realize that GOD created the world you live in and GOD is the Eternal power that keeps the world turning on its axis, so that tomorrow you can wake up again. You do not even grow hair without GOD's DNA sequence in your genes. You can see the hair and see that is growing but you have no idea what makes it grow or what forces the hair through your skin or what makes it fall out.

The complexity of the world leaves "no doubt" there is a Creator, GOD.
Listen to this beautiful praise called, "This Is My Father's World"

This is my Father's world, and to my listening ears
All nature sings, and round me rings the music of the spheres.
This is my Father's world: I rest me in the thought
Of rocks and trees, of skies and seas;
His hand the wonders wrought.

This is my Father's world, the birds their carols raise,
The morning light, the lily white, declare their Maker's praise.
This is my Father's world: He shines in all that's fair;
In the rustling grass I hear Him pass;
He speaks to me everywhere.

This is my Father's world. O let me ne'er forget
That though the wrong seems oft so strong, God is the ruler yet.
This is my Father's world: the battle is not done:
Jesus Who died shall be satisfied,
And earth and Heav'n be one.

This is my Father's world, dreaming, I see His face.
I open my eyes, and in glad surprise cry, "The Lord is in this place."
This is my Father's world, from the shining courts above,
The Beloved One, His Only Son,
Came—a pledge of deathless love.

This is my Father's world, should my heart be ever sad?
The lord is King—let the heavens ring. God reigns —
let the earth be glad.
This is my Father's world. Now closer to Heaven bound,
For dear to God is the earth Christ trod.
No place but is holy ground.

This is my Father's world. I walk a desert lone.
In a bush ablaze to my wondering gaze God makes His glory known.
This is my Father's world, a wanderer I may roam
Whate'er my lot, it matters not,
My heart is still at home.

*This is my Fathers world
A pastor from upstate New York from Lockport, New York
describing the beauty of his surroundings in the way we need to view
our Father's world.
Text: Maltbie D. Babcock

The Unseen Atomic World

When you made the choice to believe in GOD, as the Creator, your view of yourself is wrapped in the love of an eternal Father and you realize that this world was made for you, not you for the natural world. **We were planned by GOD, an act of love, not an accident of the cosmos. The world is the first evidence of GOD's love for you and unlike cosmic accidents you had parents, siblings, and the Holy Spirit to guide and provide for you as you grow from infancy to maturity.** Even if you were born to non-believing parents, the Glory of GOD's creation will amaze you and bring you to a realization that GOD created the world and mankind.

Just like our bodies, the rest of our world is a creative work of art by GOD, given to us for our enjoyment. The foundations of our earth are an infinitesimal part of a gigantic galaxy system designed by GOD. Beginning with Atoms, what is an atom? What is inside an atom? Atoms are the basic building blocks of ordinary matter. Atoms can join together to form molecules, which in turn form the elements in the objects around you.

Atoms are composed of particles called protons, electrons and neutrons. Protons carry a positive electrical charge, electrons carry a negative electrical charge and neutrons carry no electrical charge at all. The protons and neutrons cluster together in the central part of the atom, called the nucleus, and the electrons 'orbit' the nucleus. A particular atom will have the same number of protons and electrons and most atoms have at least as many neutrons as protons. Does this sound like a cosmic accident?

Protons and neutrons are both composed of other particles called quarks and gluons. Protons contain two 'up' quarks and one 'down' quark while neutrons contain one 'up' quark and two 'down' quarks.

The gluons are responsible for binding the quarks to one another. The unseen world of matter is similar to the gene building blocks of our bodies.

The genes govern the growth and features of our bodies from conception to maturity. GOD infused the Atomic set of building blocks to bring about His intended purpose in our natural world (atoms, neutrons, molecules, etc.) used to develop our natural environment. Again GOD used things that cannot be seen to produce things that can be seen and GOD's power keeps the atoms in all matter that are moving at incredible speed to be stationary in the building blocks of our worlds.

Earth
Water
Plants
Iron
Mountains and rocks
And many more

Can you envision the world operating on its own or by chance? Have you ever asked yourself, how do I calculate the number of protons, electrons, and neutrons in an atom of any of the elements in our world? Think about the conditions and matter that have to be available, in proper proportions, for these invisible building blocks to make up the visible major foundational blocks of our natural world. And the power to control the building blocks to bring about their intended purpose; producing a world full of everything we need for life and don't forget Godliness.

GOD thought of everything
(There are no adjectives grand enough
to describe GOD's design.)

The complexity of our worlds designed by GOD and the intricacy of their interaction is mind-blowing. Let us examine something we intellectually give no value, **"dirt"**; GOD has programmed the regional dirt compositions so there is a different make up of soils in each climate zone to react to the growing season and the rainfall. In other words, The Lord even designed the soils to reflect what the soil would have to do to grow a crop within the elements and time available for growing. Specifically, the design of the soil makeup is different in each climate zone; where there is more rain the soil has more drainage, in the great forest there is more clay, in the fertile valleys there is more loam, along the coasts where there is more wind there is more sand. GOD knew what was needed and designed each soil to produce the crop GOD wanted it to produce. Gen 2:7 and the LORD God formed man of the dust of the ground, and breathed into his nostrils the breath of life and man became a living being. Isn't it amazing what GOD can do with dirt?

Another elemental part of our life, we don't think about is **"Air"**, without it we could not live five minutes, we breathe in the oxygen in the air, and we exhale CO_2 which is taken in by plants for their growth. On a much larger scale, when the air hydrates and forms clouds it is moved around by moving air (wind) until the completion of the hydrogen atom and the oxygen atom produces rain and falls to the earth and brings moisture to the germination of seed bearing plants so they can start growing and on and on.

Water was part of the first creation of GOD as it is the second largest component of the earth and may be the largest component of the Heavens. **Water** is also, the largest component of our own bodies. **Water** was created before light. Take note: before the fourth day when GOD made the sun and moon to rule over the night and day there were no solar-lunar days **or time as we know it**. Scientist when exploring other planets and solar systems are always looking for **water**, for without **water** there cannot be human, animal, or plant life. To date, there is no evidence concluding positive conditions exist, that could support life on any of the planets and stars of which there may be billions or trillions. In the beginning, if anything was located where our planet is, it was not yet the earth GOD made for "Man and Woman", the earth was probably similar to the other planets except in distance from other objects. When GOD started Genesis 1:1, In the beginning, GOD created the heavens and the earth, (the earth was not able to sustain life, until GOD added water, soil, rocks, minerals, oil, and millions of other things) and Job 38-41 tells us about the engineering and development that GOD went through to design where the waters would go and where would the mountains be located, where he would store the snow and the hail, and when the seasons of the year would be. GOD designed the sun and the moon and the axis and rotation of the earth to rule over the seasons and spoke it into existence. **This place was made especially for you and me and there is no other place in the stratosphere like this place** and the new place GOD has gone to prepare for us is even better. Jesus said, "Come unto me and out of your belly's will flow rivers of living water". In a description of Heaven in Revelation, it says, that there is an everlasting flow of water from below the Throne of GOD.

The sun is always shining but we are spinning in the earth's axis away from the sun into the darkness. If the earth did not spin at 1040 miles per hour we would burn, if we were on the sunny side, or freeze, if we were on the dark side. Everything about our world is a calculation of precise detail to make our world livable and suitable for plant life. According to GOD's Word, **Light** was made before the sun and the moon, which were made to rule over the night and day. We hear from the words of Jesus in

> John 8:12 "I am the light of the world. He who follows Me shall not walk in darkness, but have the light of life. "

Revelation 22:5 also tells us that in (Heaven) the new kingdom **there shall be no night or need for the sun or a lamp, for the Lord GOD gives them light**.

If there is no darkness, the light was made for a different purpose than illumination and heat. The sun and the moon rule over the day, the night, and differentiate the seasons, but GOD is the creator of light and life. We must not allow our vision to be restricted to what we can see in the natural. In a dark room the furniture is there even if we cannot see in the dark, you can't see gravity but you can see its affects. You can't see GOD but he is still there. We need to live in the Spirit World where GOD lives, not constrained by time. Existing is living without the" Light of Life" and subject to time. When you are subject to time there is always anxiety because time is constantly running out. Eternity is only possible with GOD and with Jesus you are eternal and time is not your enemy.

  Light is not the absence of Darkness, although darkness is the absence of **light**. Jesus is light and the "light of life" and both are an integral part of every aspect of your life, both in the seen and the unseen Worlds. Darkness is not a force; darkness is just the absence of light. GOD designed the darkness and corresponding reduction in temperature to produce concentration of flavor for plant life and Human rest. Every conceivable thing that grows and produces seeds must have **light**. When you savor your food, it was Jesus that gave it life and light to grow.

You "Trust the Lord" with each breath of air, crust of bread, and drink of water you consume, without thinking about it and generally without giving credit to The Creator. You assume the air will be pure, you believe the water is clean, and you think the food you eat is good for you. You are a steward of what GOD put here for your enjoyment and in any moment of sanity, you should realize that you cannot make anything from nothing and you don't control anything that matters. **This world was created for you**, because of GOD's love. Ask any doctor if they can produce life and they will tell you "no", they can assist the functions of a body, but if the light driving the electrical impulses to the Heart goes out, the life of the body is gone. Life and our worlds come from GOD. Jesus preached on Hell 33 times and the essence of Hell is a place without light, total darkness and without rest because it has neither bottom, sides, nor top.

If you believe in the God of creation, then you realize how special you are and how loved by the Creator. **If you don't believe in creation and the Creator**, then the food we eat, water we drink, air we breathe, and everything in our lives is an accident, a happenstance. In fact, non-believers are just an accident and therefore are of no value. Atheists etc. use the world's assets, but don't make the world better, but then they don't need to make it better, because in the Atheist view there is no reward for what they do, or any reward when they die, except death. Some arrogant Atheist, evolutionists, and secularists think that they make the world a better place because they are vegetarians, or they recycle, or they don't wear furs, or they are members of Animal rights groups, or they fight to keep evolution taught in schools. But there is nothing they can do that matters in the grand scheme of running this world; they need to read Job 38-41 to see if they qualify to be GOD. Here is a small excerpt; GOD speaking to Job.

> Where were you **when I founded the earth**? Tell me, if you know so much. Do you know who determined its dimensions or who stretched the measuring line across it? On what were its bases sunk, or who laid its cornerstone, When the morning stars sang together, and all the sons of God shouted for joy?

"Who shut up the sea behind closed doors when it gushed forth from the womb, when I made the clouds its blanket and dense fog its swaddling cloth, when I made the breakers its boundary set its gates and bars, and said, 'You may come this far, but no farther; here your proud waves must stop'? Job 38

We cannot miss the enormity of GOD's power and his Creation. There is no accident in the creation of our planet and if mankind causes any changes in the world and its atmosphere, the GOD of Creation will handle any changes needed to repair man's actions.

Your belief system determines your actions.
Recently my favorite Bible teacher went on a mission trip to China. He wanted to speak on comparative religion, but was told the government wanted him to speak on ethics. It turns out that their society after many years as a communist country, who do not believe in GOD and taught atheism, China has an ethics problem. Without the concept of a Creator GOD, who made life, and therefore gives life; Truth has no consequence, fidelity no norm, existence no value, etc. Ethics do not proceed from a government that does not believe in God. The only meaning in the Chinese citizen's existence is the governments.

Do you remember, the Christmas movie, "It's a Wonderful Life" with Jimmy Stewart? The story is about a town with a wonderful Godly man and how different that town and the families would have been, if he had never lived? His brother would have died, the pharmacist would have given the wrong medicine, Uncle Billy would have gone to jail, the building and loan would have gone under and Mr. Potter would have owned everything. This story is just a glimpse of what happens when GOD is not part of a society. "Love your neighbor" is not a concept in societies founded without reverence to the Creator GOD and his creation "mankind".

The Bible confirms that
Jesus made worlds not just our earth.
There are seen and unseen worlds. (plural)

The world we see is not all there is to the World we see. It is important for us, who believe in Jesus Christ, whom we can't see, feel, or touch; living inside the Kingdom of GOD, which we can't see, feel, or touch to understand that the part of the world we can see feel and touch was made from things which are not visible. While it is hard to follow the complexity of spiritual and earthly realms of life, Eternal life came while we were alive on earth at our salvation. Spiritual acts transcend the natural world and are more real than the Earthly realm. Remember the things we see were made from things which are unseen. We **are not** human beings having a Spiritual experience. **We are Spiritual beings having a human experience. In other words, the life of a follower of Jesus is not powered by his actions but is powered by the unseen power of the Spirit. It is the Believers Love for GOD and acts of love for our neighbors that bring us to an intimate relationship with GOD that open up the unseen power of the Spiritual Kingdom of GOD.**

The following scriptures tell us about the Kingdom of GOD.
> Hebrews 11:3 By faith we understand that the **worlds** (plural) were framed by the word of God, so **that the things which are seen, were not made of things which are visible.**

This scripture is from the chapter of Hebrews recounting great acts of faith, but this scripture also confirms the construction of our world is made out of things that are not visible. Not only does this describe the spiritual world but the atomic world. Everything in your life that you see, feel, and touch is made with an atomic structure that is not solid but instead the atoms in the things you see are moving at great speed. Jesus is upholding the power to keep the atomic world in its designed operation to accomplish GOD's desired end, product, or action. Only GOD can make the atomic world moving at incredible speed be controlled and captured in the material in a chair that you can sit on.

> John 8:23 And He said to them, "You are from beneath; I am from above. **You are of this world; I am not of this world.**

In this scripture Jesus is speaking to Jewish men who do not believe in Jesus as their Messiah. Jesus is on earth when He says that he is not of this world (of men stuck in their sinful state). And believers are not of this world.

> John 18:36 Jesus answered, "**My kingdom is not of this world.**"
>
> Luke 17:20 And when he was demanded of the Pharisees, when the kingdom of God should come, he answered them and said, **The Kingdom of God cometh not with observation**: ... for, behold, <u>**the Kingdom of God is within you.**</u>

In the first scripture, Jesus is talking to Pilate, and in Luke He is speaking to the Pharisees but the thrust of both scriptures is that **the Kingdom of GOD is inside each one of us and it is a spiritual world**.

> Heb 1:1 God, who at various times and in various ways spoke in time past to the fathers by the prophets, has in these last days spoken to us by His Son, whom He has appointed heir of all things, through whom also **He made the worlds (plural);** who being the brightness of His glory and the express image of His person, and **upholding all things by the word of His power**, when He had by Himself purged our sins, sat down at the right hand of The Majesty on high,

This scripture is the essence of the Gospel and announces Jesus Christ has absolute control over the universe and all the worlds; Earthly, Spiritual and Heavenly or Atomic, Cosmic, and Spiritual.

Jesus connects us to The Spiritual World when he said,
> **" I am the God of Abraham, and the God of Isaac, and the God of Jacob? God is not the God of the dead, but of the living." Matthew 22:32**

The Bible confirms that Abraham, Isaac, and Jacob died and are no longer on Earth, in the flesh, but the fact that **they are still alive speaks to the Eternal world of the Spirit** and announces that our Spirit is Eternally alive when we are born again.

The Choice

Unlike the atomic and gene building blocks that GOD made to do His purpose which happen as GOD wills, in the earth and mankind. The Spiritual world building blocks are the unseen attributes of GOD set up to do his will, but they are activated with a free will choice by mankind.

> **…When you see with your eyes, and hear with your ears and understand in your heart and find wisdom with your mind and choose to receive the love of Almighty GOD, and are converted and I will heal you. Matthew 13:15**

This is a good place to try to understand the duality of "Spirit and Flesh", "Position and Performance", and "Relationship and Fellowship" and their interplay with our lives. Mankind is a Spirit housed in a body made of flesh. The Spirit is GOD's essence of life that was given to mankind when He made us, and after the fall the Spirit was dead in trespasses and sin. The earthly body was formed to house the Spirit because it suited the environment GOD had made for Mankind. The Spirit is part of the unseen Spiritual world and naturally the body is part of the seen world.

The Spirit is either dead in trespasses and sin or "Born Again in Christ Jesus"

If the spirit is not "Born Again" the natural body just exists, because there is no life without Jesus Christ.

At the Born again experience, Jesus ignites Eternal life in your Spirit.

Salvation or being "Born Again" by faith in Jesus Christ establishes your position (foundation or platform) with GOD. Your position in Christ is permanent or eternal. Your Fellowship with GOD (Holy Spirit) will be determined by your performance in your daily choices. Believers will be known by the evidence of the fruit of the Spirit in their lives and will suffer loss for all the works of the flesh. **Your relationship with Jesus is established**, it is your "Position in Christ" it is irrevocable, but if GOD's word does not abide in you and you don't abide in GOD your fellowship with the Holy Spirit will impede your prayer life and the power of Kingdom living.

Galatians 5 lists "**the Gifts** of the Spirit" and "**the works** of the flesh". Performing the "works of the flesh" will impede your fellowship with the Holy Spirit and will hurt your heart, as you disappoint yourself, but not affect your "Position in Christ", which is eternal.

> Gal 5:24 And they that are **Christ's have crucified the flesh** with the affections and lusts. If we live in the Spirit, let us also walk in the Spirit (love, joy, peace, longsuffering, gentleness, goodness, faith, meekness, and temperance). **Now the works of the flesh are manifest, which are emulations, wrath, strife, seditions, heresies, envying's, murders, drunkenness, reveling**, and such like:

When you read the two lists, it is easy to determine if we are walking in the Spirit or if we are following the degenerate works of our flesh. As a Believer in Jesus Christ walking after the works of the flesh will cause a break in our "Fellowship with GOD" but will not sever our "Relationship with Jesus Christ" or "Position in Christ". The visible Fruit of the Spirit are resident when we take on the image of GOD created in us in a "Born again Spirit". When "Believers" are at the Judgment seat of Christ the bible says our deeds will be judged by fire and we will suffer loss for the works that burn and will receive a crown for the deeds that are purified through the fire.

All of life is defined by our love of Almighty GOD, Creator of All.

> Mat 22:36 Master, **which is the great commandment in the law?** Jesus said unto him, **Thou shalt love the Lord thy God with all thy heart, and with all thy soul, and with all thy mind.** This is the first and great commandment. And the second is like unto it, Thou shalt love thy neighbor as thyself. On these two commandments hang all the law and the prophets.
>
> Which is the first commandment of all? And Jesus answered him, The first of all the commandments is, **Hear, O Israel; The Lord our God is one Lord: And thou shalt love the Lord thy God with all thy heart, and with all thy soul, and with all thy mind, and with all thy strength: this is the first commandment. And the second is like, namely this, Thou shalt love thy neighbor as thyself.**

Loving our Creator and Savior with all our being makes performing works of the flesh, so disappointing to our hearts. Our peace and prayer life suffer until we regain fellowship with the Holy Spirit. Thank GOD we have an Advocate with the Father and when we change our direction and reinvest in the Lord's words, immerse ourselves in our pursuit of the Holy Spirit, the peace that passes understanding fills our life.

The unseen Spiritual World

Why is it important that we gain knowledge of the parts of the world's we can't see?

1.   The easiest answer is, GOD is omnipresent (everywhere) but we can't see GOD and he wants to have a relationship with us, therefore we need to know about the unseen worlds of GOD.

2.   The Kingdom of GOD is our inheritance from Jesus Christ and the Kingdom is real and inside each of us, but unseen and to enter it we must know how.

3.   Until you start thinking about the unseen worlds, you can't imagine being part of ETERNITY. Your existence will be measured in Time, if you don't receive Eternal life from belief in Jesus Christ. And time is always running out.

4.   You cannot understand the words of Jesus that, "he is upholding all things by the word of his power", until you examine the worlds Jesus is upholding. Everything in this world is powered by DNA, Atoms, molecules and other designed building blocks of our universe; all unseen but surrounding everything and in everything we touch, see, and are.

5.   You must study the Bible to understand "How to store up treasure in Heaven"; because the treasure is unseen and it is for a place you can't see at this time.

6.   Belief and knowledge of the Kingdom of GOD gives you confidence in your prayers.

7.   We are Spiritual beings having a human experience, and therefore we must understand the Spiritual World.

Conclusion:

1. GOD is the Creator of this physical world, the Human body, the

Spiritual world, and the Heavens.

2. The patent absurdity of the evolutionist's position: If existence came from a cosmic accident, where did the knowledge to live, eat, and reproduce emanate? We have all seen babies and their helplessness. Does the cosmic accident stay around to teach the accident to eat and hunt and learn a language? And later does the cosmic accident have another accident to produce woman?

3. There is more to our worlds than we can operate with our senses; the unseen world is in control of our seen world, both Atomic and Spiritual.

4. The same Spirit that raised Jesus Christ from the dead is resident in Believers and is the unseen power we hold in the unseen world of the Spirit that operates the seen world.

Overview

1. Are you amazed at the worlds GOD created for you?

2. Have you lost touch with GOD's worlds, created for you to enjoy?

3. Do you take time each day to thank GOD for your worldly blessings?

4. Does knowing that God created the world, for you, make you feel loved?

5. Are you operating in the eternal world of the Spirit or are you consumed with the problems of you biological needs?

Chapter 2

From Here to Eternity"
is more than a movie title

Understanding the Born again Spirit will increase our knowledge of Eternity. GOD speaks to us in terms of perfection and eternal truths. Mankind's use of the terms forever, has an "expiration date" of death and cannot be confused with God's eternity which has no beginning and no end.

The Marriage covenant is the most revered covenant made in the physical world today and it is made with an expiration of "till death do us part". We are programmed in life, that there are only two things you can count on, "Death and Taxes". The Truth is that expression is far from the Truth. Jesus offers The WAY, The TRUTH, and The LIFE and all are ETERNAL. Your eternal life and its benefits started with your born again experience and are only limited by your knowledge of God's word and your relationship with GOD. So my question to everyone is "till death do us part" or "From Here to Eternity", what will you choose and what will you do then?

GOD has created for mankind, a platform for eternal life arising from the Born again experience. The platform is not constrained by time and it is retroactive to each believer's birth and goes forever. It is the believers, "Position in Christ".

Your platform or Position in Christ

Human action cannot change your Gift of Grace for Salvation.

Just like the attributes of GOD which are all perfection, eternity for the Believer is without beginning or end. Your Spirit is now eternal.

No longer does GOD look at you and see a sinner, He sees a person perfected in Jesus Christ. The platform that makes up our "Position in Jesus Christ" is eternal but our performance until our physical death or the Resurrection is made up of "The fruit of the Spirit" or "The works of the flesh". Our deeds both good and bad will be judged at the Bema seat Judgment (II Cor.5:10 & Rom. 14:10-12). Our performance after salvation will suffer loss for any "works of the flesh" and receive a reward for deeds from the "Fruit of the Spirit". And scripture indicates that Almighty GOD will give us our reward personally. The Crowns for Believers are recorded in II Timothy 2:5, 4:8, James 1:12, I Peter 5:4, and Revelation 2:10.

Now that we have entrance in to the Spiritual world we must use the unseen building blocks GOD set up to operate in the unseen Spiritual world. There is more to the Spiritual world than Salvation. To affect the seen world from the Spiritual world we must use love, joy, peace, longsuffering, patience, self-control, goodness, faith, meekness, etc. We are a new creation and we have GOD living inside us, we now activate the building blocks, through prayer, acting in faith, speaking GOD's word, and searching for GOD's will in our actions.

Till Death do us part
Is the end
For non-Believers.

Death of the Body is the great equalizer of life. When your body is required of your soul and spirit, you are left with your knowledge of GOD and your collection of good deeds done for the right reason. There is nothing of worldly value that you can take with you into your Spiritual life after death. Every person who has attended a funeral knows that when the casket is closed and is buried in the earth; it is "The End, Fini, Caput, and dead". If you did not believe in GOD, you are left with a dead body and a sinful spirit. The Bible tells us of two judgments a "Believers Judgment called the "Bema seat judgment" and the unbelievers judgment called the "White throne judgment". The invitees to the judgments tell the important fact of each judgment, one is for the believers who are being judged on the performance of their life after salvation and the other judgment is for unbelievers, who are being judged for being unbelievers. Physical death for the Believers is FREEDOM. No longer is the Spirit constrained by time and the decay of the body, but is gloriously free. Death for unbelievers is full of torment and uncertainty.

Hell is a Reality

Atheists and non-believers have convinced themselves that there is no creator GOD and so they can exist anyway they want and when they die, that is all there is to their existence. This kind of arrogance will make your existence a living hell because you will miss the love of Almighty GOD to give you his peace for this world. Jesus spoke of Hell 33 times, many more times than He spoke of Heaven. The judgment for unbelievers has degrees of torment, although scripture does not elaborate on the specifics of how terrible each level of the torment will be. Probably Hitler is having second thoughts about his choices.

Eternity is a gift

Grace and truth **came**, unmerited favor **came**, the truth of salvation **came, Eternity came in the flesh and His Name is Jesus:**
> John 1:15 When John, the Baptist, was discussing Jesus with Pharisees He saw Jesus and cried out, this is the one of whom I spake, He that cometh after me was preferred ahead of me, because he existed before me.' "We have all received from his fullness, yes, grace upon grace. For the Torah was given

through Moses; **grace and truth came through Jesus**, the Messiah. No one has ever seen God; but the only and unique Son, who is identical with God and is at the Father's side — he has made Him (GOD) known.

We have been introduced to GOD by His Son, **who is identical with GOD**. It is a gift, a key to open Eternity now. The definition of Eternity is that it cannot be stopped. When you are concentrating on Eternity you will not be sidelined by lusts of the world, lust of the eye, or the pride of life. Everything about eternity is Spiritual. Our life on earth when we are abiding with GOD is a picnic on a sunny day. There is no condemnation to those who walk after the spirit and not after the flesh. An Eternal look at any earthly problem puts our time on earth in perspective. It is our purpose to be faithful to Almighty GOD through the short lived situations we call problems and enjoy eternity with GOD. The bible says the time we are here on earth is a mere blink of the eye in comparison to Eternity with GOD. Don't ever forget Jesus gave us His Glory, on Earth, you represent the fruit of the sacrifice of Jesus Christ and you shine with his Glory. When GOD looks at the world there are billions of lights of Glory of His Son that must make GOD gratified, speaking in man's ability to describe anything for GOD.

Why didn't God come to Earth
on a white horse as a conquering King?

What kind of system, did GOD create, that the answer to man's failure was GOD had to sacrifice his son to reinstate Man's right standing with GOD? It was GOD's love and the parameters GOD built into the world system that determined how GOD would bring salvation and right standing to Mankind. GOD's justice and wrath is as perfect as GOD's grace and mercy. It is very important to our lives that we comprehend; we cannot do anything good enough to merit right standing with GOD. This is GOD's worlds and we can't bring a possession or do a deed to increase our standing before the judgment seat of Christ. **The perfection necessary for our right standing with GOD has to come from a sacrifice incredible enough to pay for the sins of the world; past, present, and future. GOD gave mankind all power over everything on the earth, above the earth, and in the earth and seas, therefore the only way to right the world is for there to be a sinless man, a second and last Adam .** Only the perfect life, and terrible death, and powerful resurrection, of Jesus Christ qualify to meet the payment of GOD's wrath and justice. Now that the sacrifice has been made and accepted by GOD, the choice to receive salvation is ours.

GOD will not force His will on you; it will be your choice. If you choose hell,
> you will have to **step over** "The Cross of Jesus Christ",
>> **disregard** "the empty tomb",
>>> **contradict** "the resurrection" and
>>>> **lie your way out of believing**
>>>>> "the Bible".

The Cross of Jesus Christ transcends time; it is part of the Spiritual world, changing the seen world with the power of the unseen world. If you choose GOD almighty and right standing through Jesus Christ, the power of the Spiritual World and the Kingdom of GOD is your new life from a sacrifice made nearly 2000 years ago.

Eternal life highlighted in Romans 12:9-21.
Let love be without hypocrisy. Abhor what is evil. Cling to what is good. Be kindly affectionate to one another with brotherly love, in honor giving preference to one another; not

lagging in diligence, fervent in spirit, serving the Lord; rejoicing in hope, patient in tribulation, continuing steadfastly in prayer; distributing to the needs of the saints, given to hospitality.

Bless those who persecute you; bless and do not curse. Rejoice with those who rejoice, and weep with those who weep. Be of the same mind toward one another.

Do not set your mind on high things, but associate with the humble. Do not be wise in your own opinion. Repay no one evil for evil. Have regard for good things in the sight of all men. If it is possible, as much as depends on you, live peaceably with all men.

Beloved, do not avenge yourselves, but rather give place to wrath; for it is written, "VENGEANCE IS MINE, I WILL REPAY," says the Lord. Therefore "IF YOUR ENEMY IS HUNGRY, FEED HIM; IF HE IS THIRSTY, GIVE HIM A DRINK; FOR IN SO DOING YOU WILL HEAP COALS OF FIRE ON HIS HEAD."

Do not be overcome by evil, but overcome evil with good.

Notice that each line touched the natural world from the Spirit and, not one request, served the needs of the natural man but was concentrated on changing the seen world from the power of the unseen world for our neighbors, ourselves, and to accomplish GOD's will on Earth as it is in Heaven. The picture of the life of our Savior is one of love and service. Your battles are not with yourself or other people; but with living in this world but not being of this world, following the Spirit and not the lusting after the flesh, resist the enemy and stay faithful to GOD, choose to render good for evil.

When you have a word from the Lord there is a zeal and courage in your soul that all the forces in the world cannot prevail against. And you have a word from the Lord: seek first the Kingdom of GOD.

There are battles to be fought in the Kingdom, but GOD is there to fight for us. Let us take a minute to look at Joshua entering the Promised Land to see the similarities to our entering the Kingdom of GOD. There may be giants in our land that we have to defeat or chase out of our land but GOD is with us to give us the victory. Believers have been given the platform of Eternal life and from this platform high above the world of sin we battle for our "thought life". **Our belief system determines our actions**. Notice GOD tells Joshua to "be strong and of good courage" three times in this chapter. We need to be in touch with GOD, all the time, to operate our life inside the Kingdom of GOD. It took this belief in GOD for Joshua to bring his thoughts captive so that GOD's power could win the battles he would face.

> Jos 1:1 After the death of Moses the servant of the LORD, it came to pass that the LORD spoke to Joshua the son of Nun, Moses' assistant, saying: "Moses My servant is dead. **Now therefore, "arise, go" over this Jordan**, you and all this people, to the land which I am giving to them—the children of Israel. Every place that the sole of your foot will tread upon I have given you, as I said to Moses. From the wilderness and this Lebanon as far as the great river, the River Euphrates, all the land of the Hittites, and to the Great Sea toward the going down of the sun, shall be your territory. No man shall be able to stand before you all the days of your life; as I was with Moses, so I will be with you. I will not leave you nor forsake you. **Be strong and of good courage**, for to this people you shall divide as an inheritance the land

which I swore to their fathers to give them. Only **be strong and very courageous**, that you may observe to do according to all the law which Moses My servant commanded you; do not turn from it to the right hand or to the left, that you may prosper wherever you go. **This Book of the Law shall not depart from your mouth, but you shall meditate in it day and night, that you may observe to do according to all that is written in it. For then you will make your way prosperous, and then you will have good success.** Have I not commanded you? **Be strong and of good courage**; do not be afraid, nor be dismayed, for the LORD your God is with you wherever you go." Then Joshua commanded the officers of the people, saying, "Pass through the camp and command the people, saying, 'Prepare provisions for yourselves, for within three days you will cross over this Jordan, **to go in to possess the land which the LORD your God is giving you to possess.'**

When GOD Almighty told Joshua to cross the Jordan, the river was at flood stage, the pillar of cloud by day and the pillar of fire by night were gone, the daily manna supply had stopped and there were giants in the land. If you did not have History with GOD and a word from The Almighty, it would have been a very fearful experience. All believers have a word from GOD to enter the Kingdom of GOD.

Remember, when Joshua told the Levites to carry the Ark of the Covenant into the flooding Jordan River, when the first foot hit the water, the waters separated and several million Israelites crossed the flooding river into the Promised Land on dry ground, all passing by the Ark of the Covenant stationed in the middle of the Jordan River. The mathematics for two million plus people to pass through the Jordan River in one day would necessitate a crossing path of at least one mile. Joshua believed in GOD's word and GOD gave them their inheritance. Israel had to fight to take the Promised Land, but GOD was with them and gave them the victory. As a memorial to the Passing through the Jordan, a man from each tribe took a boulder from where the Ark stood to shore and brought twelve boulders to the place where the Ark stood in the middle of the Jordan and stacked them up as a sign.

Take Note, Joshua walked around the city of Jericho for seven days, blew trumpets and the walls fell down and the people surrendered. We cannot let anything prevent us from having a wonderful intimate relationship with Father God, He has prepared the way, He will fight our battles, just ask HIM.

<u>**Why are we here?**</u>
<u>**and**</u>
<u>**What is our purpose?**</u>

GOD brought all the creatures on earth before Adam and he named all the creatures. Adam could not find a suitable mate from all the created beings on earth and was incomplete or lonely, and so GOD put Adam to sleep and took one of Man's ribs and made Woman (Genesis 2:20-22). It seems reasonable to deduce from the Bible, and its symbolism that GOD looked at all his creations and GOD's quest for an intimate loving relationship and it was not complete. And then, GOD made a creature in His own image that could return love of a free will. Mankind, like the rib used to make woman, was made for relationship with GOD. I believe GOD looked around the created Kingdom of GOD and could not find a suitable mate or companion and so He took of Himself and fashioned man (and woman), in His own image. Adam separated himself from GOD with his rejection of their covenant. **The ultimate act of love was GOD's provision to restore the covenant, God had made, with Mankind and man had** broken. It did not cost GOD anything to create the sun, stars, earth and everything on earth but it cost GOD everything to save one life by sacrificing part of Himself. It is now incumbent on us to enter the Kingdom of GOD and "live in the Spirit" not "exist in the flesh".

Jesus has made us Kings and Priests

Rev 1:4 John, to the seven churches which are in Asia: Grace to you and peace from **Him who is,** and **who was**, and **who is to come**, and from the seven Spirits who are before His throne, and from Jesus Christ, the faithful witness, the firstborn from the dead, and the ruler over the kings of the earth. **To Him who loved us and washed us from our sins in His own blood**, and **has made us kings and priests to His God and Father, to Him be glory and dominion forever and ever. Amen.**
Jesus is the King of Kings and we are the Kings, and Jesus is the High Priest and we are the Priests.

Jesus has made us Holy and separated for GOD.

(Heb 10:7) Then I said, 'Look! In the scroll of the book it is written about me. I have come to do your will.' " In saying first, "You neither willed nor were pleased with animal sacrifices, meal offerings, burnt offerings and sin offerings," things which are offered in accordance with the Torah; and then, "Look, I have come to do your will"; H**e (Jesus) takes away the first system in order to set up the second. It is in connection with this will that we have been separated for God and made holy, once and for all, through the offering of Jesus, the Messiah's body**. Now every Priest (Not preaching Jesus Crucified)stands every day doing his service, offering over and over the same sacrifices, which can never take away sins.

GOD Almighty remembers our sins no more and an offering for sins is no longer needed.

> (Heb 10:12) But this one (Jesus, The Messiah), after he had offered for all time a single sacrifice for sins, sat down at the right hand of God, from then on to wait until his enemies be made a footstool for his feet. For by a single offering he (Jesus, The Messiah) has brought to the goal, for all time, those who are being set apart for God and made holy. And the Ruach HaKodesh (Holy Spirit) too bears witness to us; for after saying, " 'This is the covenant which I will make with them after those days,' says Adonai: 'I will put my (instructions) Torah on their hearts, and write it on their minds . . . ,' " **he then adds, " 'And their sins and their wickednesses I will remember no more.' " Now where there is forgiveness for these, an offering for sins is no longer needed.**

The Priests could not sit down in the Temple, because their work was never done, but Jesus finished the work and sat down at the right hand of the Father. **NOW WHEN OUR ACCOUNT IS EXAMINED THE BALANCE SAYS "PAID IN FULL".**

Here is a song that describes the person who does not realize or acknowledge that there is a Creator GOD and our need for a Savior.

What kind of fool am I?
Who never needed GOD?
It seems that I'm the only one
That I have been thinking of,

When will I see my life,
For what it really is,
An empty shell in which

A lonely heart must dwell.

What kind of life is this
Why am I here
I want to know the truth
Don't leave me alone like this

What kind of love has he,
who sent His Son for me
that fellowship with HIM
might be restored for you and for me,

O what kind of GOD is this,
HE sent HIS SON,
The only sacrifice, In Him, all sin is gone,
What kind of love has HE,

Who went to Calvary
To heal the sick and broken hearted,
And to set the captive free
What Kind of love is this

Who never gave up on me
It seems that I'm the one
That GOD has been thinking of,
O What kind of GOD is this?

In today's World of entertainment, Talent is worth the most money.
If you can add character to talent you have the best of the material
world. Tiger Woods' talent plus perceived character was worth a
billion dollars but when his character failed he was only worth what
his talent was worth.

In today's world of Jesus Christ, salvation is the most valuable. If you add an intimate relationship with GOD, you have the best of both material and Spiritual worlds and you can't lose what Jesus Christ has done for you. You have GOD's love and eternal life and are an heir of all things.

You must believe, and have faith to use
the invisible attributes of GOD
to control the seen world from the unseen Spiritual world.

Jesus healed the sick, cleansed the lepers, raised the dead, comforted the brokenhearted, fed the thousands, preached the Gospel to the poor, changed the water to wine, **and told all believer's that we would do greater works than these because Jesus was going to the Father.** The greatest thing we can do is the resurrection of a dead spirit to a born again believer in Jesus Christ by the word of our testimony and the discipline of our lives.

Notes

Chapter 3

Happiness will never come to those
who don't appreciate
what they have.

Listen to this story about a man in a terrible situation in the words of
a 12th Century poet about considering your circumstances;

"I never complained of the vicissitudes of fortune, nor
suffered my face to be overcast at the revolution of the heavens,
except once, when my feet were bare, and I had not the means of
obtaining shoes. I came to the chief of Kufah in a state of much
dejection, **and saw there a man who had no feet**. I returned thanks
to God and acknowledged his mercies, and endured my want of shoes
with patience."

Don't allow yourself to be overwhelmed by the problem causing you
to miss your goal, without consulting Almighty GOD to understand
if your goal and GOD's goal are the same. You may have missed
your goal but pleased GOD with how you lived through the
experience and therefore accomplished GOD's goal for you. No
possession on earth will mean anything in your spiritual life, only
faithfulness pleases GOD. (Hebrews 11:6)

Those who appreciate what they have, and the Creator, Who made it,
will live in joy, unspeakable. Happiness is a spiritual fulfillment; it
is not the same as the non-believers conditional status of well-fed,
well-dressed or naked and hungry etc. When a non-believer is hungry
and finds a tree and picks some fruit and eats, the status of the non-
believer is full of food, but hunger will return. When the child of
GOD ask for his daily bread in his morning prayers and finds the
same tree and picks some fruit and eats and is filled, he worships
God and is filled with happiness and with food. Everything in the

believers life can be Spiritual or carnal. In the book of Philippians, Paul receiving money and goods from the Philippians describes their carnal gifts as being changed to a spiritual reward, so again money and food stuffs when given away in love to help the needy become Spiritual and bring happiness to the giver and receiver.

Php 4:4 Rejoice in the Lord always: and again I say, Rejoice. Let your moderation be known unto all men. The Lord is at hand. Be careful for nothing; but in everything by prayer and supplication with thanksgiving let your requests be made known unto God. **And the peace of God, which passeth all understanding, shall keep your hearts and minds through Christ Jesus.** Finally, brethren, whatsoever things **are true**, whatsoever things **are honest**, whatsoever things **are just**, whatsoever things **are pure**, whatsoever things **are lovely**, whatsoever things **are of good report**; if there be any virtue, and if there be any praise, **think on these things**. Those things, which ye have both learned, and received, and heard, and seen in me, do: and the God of peace shall be with you. But I rejoiced in the Lord greatly, that now at the last your care of me hath flourished again; wherein ye were also careful, but ye lacked opportunity**. Not that I speak in respect of want: for I have learned, in whatsoever state I am, therewith to be content**. I know both how to be abased, and I know how to abound: everywhere and in all things I am instructed both to be full and to be hungry, both to abound and to suffer need. **I can do all things through Christ which strengtheneth me.**

What consumes the majority of your thinking? We shout for joy when one of our children bring home a great report card or are successful in a sporting event or excel in a piano recital. But Joy is more than watching our children excelling at an endeavor; although it does bring a smile to our faces. We teach our children, and our families, to have the best, drive the best, go to the best college, get the best job, but these teachings while enabling our families to prosper in the natural world; fall woefully short of teaching our families how to be successful in all the worlds we live in. We must add to the teachings for this world the more important teachings of the Spiritual world: forgiveness, empathy, love, caring, giving and more. Our actions identify the Spirit of GOD in our life or the lack thereof. There are no mundane activities of the day in an intimate walk with GOD. Take the time to think about God and all he has made to enrich your life, it never gets old talking to The Creator of the worlds. Believers can talk to God all day every day and if you listen, the Holy Spirit will lead and communicate with you. An intimate relationship with GOD is our goal and Heaven is our prize. Isaiah 6:3

The instructions given us by GOD are to teach our family to love GOD with all our hearts and to love our neighbor as ourselves. Don't judge others, have empathy, praise GOD, and pray all the time, while going around doing good. Knowledge of GOD and relationship with GOD allow you to be a part of the seen and the unseen worlds, simultaneously. You may be thinking that I have gone off the deep end and no one can think about GOD all day and you may be right. But my own experience confirms, that there are times when I don't think about GOD all the time, but when I don't think about GOD, I need forgiveness, or to say I am sorry, or change the direction of my mind from the lust of the world, or resist when anger rises in my being, or to remember my GOD when I am afraid. Thank GOD, in that moment of uncertainty, I know that my attitude of praise to GOD has gone by the wayside, I can quote a scripture or sing a praise and be back in an attitude of praise and re-enter GOD's rest and direction by talking to GOD.

Listen to this story about praise in 2 Chronicles 20:18-22 King Jehoshaphat sent praisers in front of his armies and GOD gave them the victory. Would you ever send the choir in front of the army?

And Jehoshaphat bowed his head with his face to the ground, and all Judah and the inhabitants of Jerusalem bowed before the LORD, worshiping the LORD. Then the Levites of the children of the Kohathites and of the children of the Korahites stood up to praise the LORD God of Israel with voices loud and high. So they rose early in the stood and said, "Hear me, O Judah and you inhabitants of Jerusalem: Believe in the LORD your GOD and you shall be established; believe His prophets, and you shall prosper, **and who should praise the beauty of holiness, as they went out before the army and were saying: "Praise the LORD**." And when he had consulted with the people, he appointed those who should sing to the LORD, For His mercy endures forever." Now when they began to sing and to praise, the LORD set ambushes against the people of Ammon, Moab, and Mount Seir, who had come against Judah; and they were defeated.

In the same way that Jehoshaphat sent praisers ahead of his army we must send praises ahead of anything keeping us from entering the promised land of the Kingdom of God. Praises to God don't change the situation you are facing but it changes the way you look at the situation you are facing and it opens up the power of the unseen world to control the seen world.

The power of praise keeps your heart in an attitude toward GOD Almighty.
The power to enter into the Kingdom of GOD and its reciprocal of GOD abiding in us is to praise and acknowledge GOD for who He is. Praise GOD for everything around us from the air we breathe, our nation with its prosperity, our family, a GOD that loves us. It is not

the noise of verbalizing praise and acknowledging GOD, that accomplishes intimacy with GOD, it is the "attitude of the heart" that assures that the intimacy of relationship is reciprocal. Again thoughts can be carnal or spiritual and it is up to you to eliminate carnal thoughts and concentrate on spiritual thoughts.

Believe it or not, **you need to serve GOD to make yourself happy.** How can serving GOD make me happy? Doesn't serving GOD mean doing something I don't want to do? The answer is no. Filling your existence with activities that feel good, taste good, and look good, vanish soon after their completion and don't lead to happiness. Only good deeds done from a heart of love will last through today and into forever. Every society and individual wants to know and understand their purpose? Only in a heart based on a "GOD created world" can we find our purpose. Loving your Savior with all your heart and loving your neighbor as yourself, brands a life with caring about your fellow man and that life is full of heartwarming acts of kindness that will fill you with happiness.

Think about a society based on evolution and man coming from a cosmic accident. **Without GOD in your society there are only conditions of status**, for example; well fed, well dressed, well-armed, or hungry, parched, or naked. In a society where your presence is presumed to be a cosmic accident and you are the highest life form; the future is today and what you can make of it. There are no ethics or morals inbred in a cosmic accident and therefore no leadership to direct man on learning to eat and what to eat and how to establish families, tribes, societies, and governments. Whatever you have and whatever you are is subject to the meaner, nastier person or group, who will take what you have and destroy who you are.

It is the fact; we have a Creator GOD that gives hope for a future. You may ask why? The answer is, if you have a creator, you have self-value, someone wanted you, you were made for a purpose and you have choices. **If you are an accident** then there is no love in a cosmic accident to give you purpose, no one to look up to for guidance, no family, and no knowledge of life. You will step into a world without knowledge of GOD, language, size, education, and culture. Self-preservation will be the norm and fear will be out of control. Instead of being eternal, you will be existing against the clock and there will never be enough hours in the day.

What is the level of the Knowledge of GOD in your heart?

Jesus has made us Kings and Priests (Rev. 1:6, 5:10) and there are requirements for our vocations. Listen to the requirements for being a King. Have you written your own copy of the Bible?

One of GOD's requirements for being a King is to write his own copy of the bible.

> Deu 17:14 When thou art come unto the land which the LORD thy God giveth thee,   and shalt possess it, and shalt dwell therein, and shalt say, I will set a king over me, like as all the nations that are about me; Thou shalt in any wise set him king over thee, whom the LORD thy God shall choose: one from among thy brethren shalt thou set king over thee: thou mayest not set a stranger over thee, which is not thy brother.
>
> But he shall not multiply horses to himself, nor cause the people to return to Egypt, to the end that he should multiply horses: forasmuch as the LORD hath said unto you, Ye shall henceforth return no more that way. Neither shall he multiply

wives to himself, that his heart turn not away: neither shall he greatly multiply to himself silver and gold. **And it shall be, when he sitteth upon the throne of his kingdom, that he shall write him a copy of this law in a book (Bible) out of that which is before the priests the Levites: And it shall be with him, and he shall read therein all the days of his life: that he may learn to fear the LORD his God, to keep all the words of this law and these statutes, to do them: That his heart be not lifted up above his brethren, and that he turn not aside from the commandment, to the right hand, or to the left: to the end that he may prolong his days in his kingdom, he, and his children, in the midst of Israel.**

When we choose a direction for our career we dedicate ourselves to obtaining the knowledge necessary to accomplish that career. When we choose to develop an intimate relationship with GOD, it is incumbent on us to obtain the knowledge of the Word of GOD necessary to be able to accomplish our prayer life and communication with GOD. Jesus when he was a baby was not a full grown man, he was a baby, He could not feed himself, He did not know how to speak a language, He did not know the Torah, His relationship with GOD was just beginning. Listen to this scripture from Luke:

Luke 2:52 And Jesus grew both in wisdom and in stature, gaining favor both with other people and with God.

Believers must grow in knowledge of GOD and communication (prayers) with GOD to grow in favor with people and GOD.

The relationship with GOD is unseen with the eye, but seen with the heart. Only your knowledge of GOD and interaction with GOD will transcend the physical world. You are going to leave this world, naked of the goals accomplished, houses bought, cars collected, and college degrees held. GOD wants to have an intimate relationship with each one of us, and GOD promises prosperity, in the world of the heart and the seen world, to everyone that loves GOD with all his heart, soul, and strength. Similar to the instructions to Moses and Joshua; the third proverb describes how to live and cultivate an intimate relationship with GOD. The third proverb details the instructions necessary for peace and fulfillment and identifies Wisdom and Understanding as being the personification of Jesus Christ, which we can have resident in our lives, if we search and find it.

Part 1 of third Proverb. **Instructions for living a fulfilling life**

Pro 3:1 My son, do not forget my (instructions) law, But let your heart keep my commands; For length of days and long life and peace they will add to you. Let not mercy and truth forsake you; Bind them around your neck, Write them on the tablet of your heart, And so find favor and high esteem In the sight of God and man. Trust in the LORD with all your heart, And lean not on your own understanding; In all your ways acknowledge Him, And He shall direct your paths.

Pro 3:7 Do not be wise in your own eyes; Fear the LORD and depart from evil. It will be health to your flesh, And strength to your bones. Honor the LORD with your possessions, And with the first fruits of all your increase; So your barns will be filled with plenty, And your vats will overflow with new wine. My son, do not despise the chastening of the LORD, Nor detest His correction; For whom the LORD loves He corrects, Just as a father the son in whom he delights.

Part 2 of the Third Proverb. **Beginning of Wisdom**
Notice that the pronouns changed in verse 14 from he to her and from here to the end of part 2 of the proverb, wisdom and understanding

is female after the man finds her (wisdom and understanding). Certainly this applies in marriage, but for this study I want to emphasize that **when man or woman finds the spiritual (unseen) part of GOD and acknowledges The Creator, the relationship begins. You were designed to fellowship with GOD and without a daily dialogue you will not receive the love available nor the satisfaction of the love you have to give.** Wisdom and understanding is Jesus Christ. Christianity is not for dummies, we must expand our knowledge of GOD.

> **Proverbs 3:13 Happy is the man who finds wisdom, And the man who gains understanding;** For her proceeds are better than the profits of silver, And her gain than fine gold. She is more precious than rubies, And all the things you may desire cannot compare with her. Length of days is in her right hand, In her left hand riches and honor. Her ways are ways of pleasantness, And all her paths are peace. She is a tree of life to those who take hold of her, And happy are all who retain her. The LORD by wisdom founded the earth; By understanding He established the heavens; By His knowledge the depths were broken up, And clouds drop down the dew.

Re-read and store in your heart everything that having a relationship with Jesus means to you and your life, health, and fulfillment and it comes from wisdom and understanding.

Part 3 of the Third Proverb. **Continuation of instructions for living a fulfilling life;**

> Pro 3:21 My son, let them not depart from your eyes— Keep sound wisdom and discretion; So they will be life to your soul And grace to your neck. Then you will walk safely in your way, and your foot will not stumble. When you lie down, you will not be afraid; yes, you will lie down and your sleep will be sweet.

Notice that the Do nots, are positive instructions written in the negative for us to maintain GOD's peace and not fall into fear,

> **Proverbs 3:25 Do not** be afraid of sudden terror, Nor of trouble from the wicked when it comes;For the LORD will be your confidence, And will keep your foot from being caught. **Do not** withhold good from those to whom it is due, when it is in the power of your hand to do so. **Do not** say to your neighbor, "Go, and come back, and tomorrow I will give it," When you have it with you. **Do not** devise evil against your neighbor, for he dwells by you for safety's sake**. Do not** strive with a man without cause, if he has done you no harm. **Do not** envy the oppressor, and choose none of his ways; for the perverse person is an abomination to the LORD, but His secret counsel is with the upright. The curse of the LORD is on the house of the wicked; But He blesses the home of the just. Surely He scorns the scornful, but gives grace to the humble. The wise shall inherit glory, but shame shall be the legacy of fools.

When you have a relationship with GOD the DNA in your body changes for the better? The curse of sin in the flesh has been condemned by GOD and therefore you are a new creature. The average life span for a Christian is significantly longer than a non-believer. Stress is the killer of the body and GOD's rest is the medicine. There are several studies working to prove this fact and I believe it will be proven, although the liberal scientist will fight this to "their death". When sin entered the world the lamb and the lion ate grass together, roses did not have thorns, snakes did not produce poison, and man did not know death. Something changed in everything on earth.

**Your belief system
determines
your actions.**

We can, in the words of the bible,

"Trust in the Lord with all your heart and lean not to our own understanding. Prov 3:5 or as Jesus said, "Therefore do not worry, saying, 'What shall we eat?' or 'What shall we drink?' or 'What shall we wear?' For after all these things the Gentiles seek. For your heavenly Father knows that you need all these things. **But seek first the kingdom of God and His righteousness, and all these things shall be added to you. Matt 6:30-32**

It is not logical to our sense driven world to involve the supernatural provision of GOD in our daily life but it is the instruction Jesus has given us, use the unseen world to bring about things needed in the seen world. "Give us this day our daily bread" is the Lord's instruction on prayer. Just to name one.

The power to change hearts comes from GOD
When Believers give these attributes of GOD their proper significance we will operate in Power:

We know that GOD is love, but we have cheapened the word and do not equate it with the love that consumed Abraham when he started to sacrifice his son to GOD. The first time the word love is used in the Bible.

We know that GOD is truth, but we don't realize the enormity of TRUTH. It is more than the opposite of a lie. The entire world operates on GOD's Truth. Truth is the perfection of the completion of the attributes of GOD. Jesus came in Grace and Truth.

We know that GOD is good and we think we are good, but when Jesus Christ was called good, even Jesus said "There is only one that is good and that is GOD". Good is a description of the Attributes of GOD in their perfection. It is also an attribute that is part of the Spiritual world not the Physical world until believers are in the Kingdom of GOD.

We know that GOD is Peace or Shalom but the word peace is not absence of war, but closer to the word, shalom which means complete well-being. There are scientific studies being done to show that a Christians DNA changes with the elimination of the curse and the indwelling of GOD in our bodies and the birth of our Eternal Spirit.

Jesus did not just die for the sins of Christians, but of every person who has ever existed and will ever exist, even if they don't choose to believe in Jesus Christ. Jesus sacrifice was perfect in its payment for GOD's perfect justice. It takes faith in Jesus Christ to alter our life and GOD's grace makes us a new creation. **It is that belief** that is so powerful that it powers your resurrection from dead in trespasses and sins to alive with Eternal life in Jesus Christ.

Thoughts and intentions of the heart
Of people who are their own god.

Here is a quote attributed to Comedian George Carlin at the end of his existence. This quote is a disheartening description of someone who exists for themselves and does not know or care about GOD.

"We drink too much, smoke too much, Laugh too little,
Drive too fast, get too angry, and stay up too late,
Get up too tired, read too little, Watch TV too much.
We have multiplied our possessions but reduced our values.
We talk too much, love too seldom, and hate too often.
We've learned how to make a living but not a life,
We have added years to life, not life to years."

When you hear a lament about one's existence like this one attributed to comedian George Carlin, you can see the result of an existence without hope. He made a good living but wanted a GOOD life. His words cry out for meaning, which cannot be found in an existence centered on our physiological needs and the pleasures of our hands.

Atheist view of existing, **"existing is a reason and a result unto itself".**

Another quote from a book trying to explore the meaning of life and written from the atheist point of view, the book is a 4 act play called

"The last person to see Farrokh". The intro states,
"There is nowhere to go, and nowhere to come back from. We are all living in a dream, in an infinite number of worlds that we have dreamt of". As dusk falls over a desert landscape, a lone woman waits anxiously. Her quest? "To find someone who is not, someone who does not exist". The search for Farrokh is a journey through fundamental human experience; confusion, aspiration, doubt, belief, submission, rebellion, love, money, power, and beyond all, our eternal question: why? A play in the tradition of Camus, Beckett, and Genet; "The Last Person Who Saw Farrokh" illuminates a path that would take us from the confusion of "why" to the clarity of "how", from the Ape of Reason to the Superman of Will. Romance with confusion "Will to Power," not reason, should be our guide to ultimate "Knowledge." "Life is-a reason and result unto itself".

Notice that this kind of existence has no hope. The first line "nowhere to go and no where to come back from." And the last line "life is a reason and a result unto itself".

GOD gives us purpose
During the Second World War the Italians praised Mussolini for making the trains run on time. Take a minute to think what it takes for GOD to make the universe run on time. The earth to spin on its axis at 1040 miles per hour, the clouds to interact with the sun to heat

the earth and maintain a temperature that humans can live and plants will grow, and millions of other requirements for life. The power to uphold the universe, scripture tells us, is in the hand of our Savior, Jesus Christ. And Jesus has made and is supervising all of these parts of our life to create the worlds for our pleasure until he comes again.

Detractors from a "GOD created world", are stuck on small minded thinking, for example; Green peace, Peta, Global warming, evolutionists, to name a few. This is how small minded they are; Green peace constituents exalt Nature as their god when it is GOD that made nature. If man destroys part of nature, God can make more. When the Chinese government decided that the song birds ate too much of their crops they killed the songbirds and then the locusts, that the songbirds also ate, destroyed their crops. After the songbirds re-multiplied balance was restored. PETA, people for the ethical treatment of animals do not want people to wear furs, or the use of animals as test subjects for medicine, but it was GOD who supplied Adam and Eve with the first fur coats and the first blood sacrifice. In most states, the animals that are approved for hunting are killed to bring the population of the species within the food supply available, so the animals don't starve. The animals were put on earth for our pleasure, food, and offerings.

Global Warming advocates think "man" can fix something that GOD made which is not broken but is working according to GOD's plan. If it were to need correction only GOD has the ability to change the world. Ask yourself what can you do to affect your neighborhood let alone the world or the cosmos. Evolutionists believe we are an accident of nature, but when scientists and uneducated people look at this creation, we know there is a creator GOD. This world and these bodies are no accident.

This is GOD's word to Noah and his descendants, of which you are one.

So God blessed Noah and his sons, and said to them: "Be fruitful and multiply, and fill the earth. And the fear of you and the dread of you shall be on every beast of the earth, on every bird of the air, on all that move on the earth, and on all the fish of the sea. **They are given into your hand. Every moving thing that lives shall be food for you. I have given you all things, even as the green herbs.** But you shall not eat flesh with its life, that is, its blood (don't eat animals that have been strangled). Genesis 9

Mankind in union with GOD is the most powerful force for GOOD in the universe and it will be best if we leave the Cosmos stuff to GOD.

The first commandment is the foundation for complete well-being.

Loving GOD with all your heart must be the foundation of life for a Believer. Praise to GOD with worship for His Being and His Creation must fill our heart to overflowing and our goal is to go about doing good.

The Lord's model prayer; **OUR FATHER, Which art in Heaven, Hallowed be thy name.**

Jesus when teaching us to pray has the perfect example of love and honor and praise in the first ten words of the Lord's Prayer. Take note, we are the only creature on earth that can love GOD and praise Him for who He is and what He has done and will do. You may be asking, "what about my job, watching television, driving the kids to school, and things that take time out of every day?" GOD's creative power is alive in everything we touch, see, hear, smell, or taste. You can live inside an attitude of praise and acknowledging GOD. GOD is there with you every minute of every day, because of His Omnipresence. GOD made everything that you care about, not only your spouse and children, but the world we live in:

Incredible Solar system

Beautiful Atmosphere

Wonderful Earth

Unbelievable Body

Spiritual World

Right standing with our GOD through Jesus Christ

Heaven and Eternity.

If you are awestruck by your GOD and His gifts to you, then you will thrive in an attitude of thanksgiving and acknowledgment and the result will be entering the peace of GOD through controlling the seen world through the power of the Spiritual world. Not accepting credit for the good things you do or say, will help you keep GOD's perspective. Your view of yourself will be trusting toward GOD who cares about you and provided this world and the one to come just for you.

Consider what GOD does for you every morning at the unfolding of a new day, the light of dawn streaking across the heavens, illuminating everywhere it goes; revealing the configuration of the earth's surface, and bringing out the colors of the dawn, inspiring all of mankind and giving man a canvas upon which to paint his day. What do you think about when you arise for the day? Try to imagine yourself in the attributes of GOD, which in their perfectness are beautiful: trust, grace, peace, mercy, power, love, and more. And using the invisible building blocks of the unseen world of the Spirit of GOD to control situations in the seen world.

If you woke up and did not notice the new day and its Creator, if you are preoccupied with your busy schedule then your "view of yourself" is as the provider and your view of GOD, is "GOD is irrelevant to your existence". If you are the "head person in charge" in your existence and family, then your view of yourself, is racked with questions of providing food, clothing, shelter, and security. Therefore, you are existing in this world in your own power, with only yourself to consult with and pray to for help. A very lonely existence.

The Christian life is not without situations we refer to as problems. Each life will have situations, that are not meeting the goals that you have set for yourself and your family, but GOD does not judge you on whether you meet your goals, or if you amass degrees or houses, or money, but whether you were faithful to loving GOD with all your heart and loving your neighbor as yourself through your situations. Two great men in the Bible, Paul and Joseph spent time in jail and many other harrowing experiences but were successful in the world and in GOD's eyes.

> Paul said, "as far as I am concerned, I have learned to be content regardless of circumstances. I know what it is to be in want, and I know what it is to have more than enough — in everything and in every way I have learned the secret of being full and being hungry, of having abundance and being in need. I can do all things through him who gives me power". Phillipians 4:11-13

All of us can be content at the end of the day if we lived the day with GOD as the focus of our heart. Because Man does not live by bread alone but by every word that proceeds from the mouth of GOD. Notice, in all these thoughts and situations the unseen world of the Spirit is ruling over the seen world of the flesh.

Right believing leads to right living but right living will not increase to right believing. GOD DOES NOT REWARD YOU FOR THE ACCUMULATION OF ASSETS, OR DEGREES, OR TROPHIES, BUT FOR FAITHFULNESS AND RIGHT BELIEVING. Inside an abiding life with GOD there is peace, and complete wellbeing. This is wellbeing of the heart and soul stretching out from the unseen world to the seen world. GOD is the "supply" of wellbeing through belief not the "demand" for righteousness through actions. If you love GOD with all your heart, your actions will be driven by your love. Consciously meditate on the Love of God "**for you**" and that love will make you want to be a better person.

The building blocks of the Spiritual Kingdom of GOD are the Fruit of the Spirit

The song "All you need is love" is correct because **God is love**, but there is even more of GOD than love. Believers seeking the Kingdom of GOD are only limited by our knowledge of, perception of, and interaction with God.

Proverbs 23:7 as a man thinketh in his heart, so is he.
The Bible constantly speaks to us about the spiritual world; the world we must embrace with our heart (soul). Like the atoms of the seen world the Fruit of the Spirit is inside your heart and unseen. The Fruit of the Spirit are the building blocks to a relationship with GOD and the power to change the seen world.

> Gal 5:22 But the fruit of the Spirit is love, joy, peace, longsuffering, gentleness, goodness, faith, Meekness, temperance: against such there is no law.

Eph 5:9 (For the fruit of the Spirit is in all goodness and righteousness and truth;) Proving what is acceptable unto the Lord.

The fruit of the Spirit is a picture of the Eternal part of our lives and are the attributes of GOD. You can't see the fruit of the Spirit but you can feel it with your heart. Without the fruit of the Spirit resident in your actions you cannot be acting in the will of GOD.
It is easy to see the differences in actions when the "Fruit of the Spirit of God" is compared to the "works of the flesh";

> Now the works of the flesh are manifest, which are these; Adultery, fornication, uncleanness, lasciviousness, Idolatry, witchcraft, hatred, variance, emulations, wrath, strife, seditions, heresies, Envyings, murders, drunkenness, revellings, Galatians 5:21

All of these actions hurt your brother or sister and are not the will of GOD and are against everything GOD has for us. Living in the Kingdom of GOD means not fulfilling the works of the flesh but acting from a heart of LOVE.

LOVE is one of GOD's attributes and it may be the most beautiful. In addition to praising GOD we need to allow the love of GOD to be evident in the way we treat the people around us as a tribute to our GOD, a real emotion that comes from our heart (Soul). Love is also one of the most powerful unseen forces. We need to be the best example of "the love of GOD" given to us by Jesus Christ. In every endeavor; job, husband, father, wife, mother, friend, benefactor, and more; we can approach every situation with love in our heart. **When GOD's love was perfected HE sacrificed HIS SON for us.** Now it is our responsibility to perfect our attribute of love and do unto others as has been done unto us.

1Co 2:9 But as it is written: "EYE HAS NOT SEEN, NOR EAR HEARD, NOR HAVE ENTERED INTO THE HEART OF MAN THE THINGS WHICH GOD HAS PREPARED FOR THOSE WHO   LOVE HIM." **But God has revealed them to us through His Spirit**. For the Spirit searches all things, yes, the deep things of God.

This extraordinary promise, to believers that love GOD, gives a small glimpse of the love GOD has for us. And because it is revealed by the Holy Spirit, **the promise is for now.**

What has the Holy Spirit revealed to you? If you cannot name something, then increase your request to the Holy Spirit to reveal the deep things of GOD that GOD has prepared for you. Don't allow a comfortable existence in the flesh, to keep you from the incredible life in the Spirit. Existing in the luxury of a rich American household, masks the need for eternal life in the Kingdom of GOD and is the epitome of the Lord's words,

> "It is more difficult for a Camel to go through the eye of a needle than a rich man to enter the Kingdom of GOD." Matthew 19:24

We must not allow meeting our daily needs with resources, that GOD has given us, to be assumed to be ours. Believers and unbelievers did not make anything without using GOD's materials and mental powers and meeting our physiological needs is not life, it is existing. Existing will give you up to 80, 90, or 100 years but living in the Spiritual Kingdom of GOD will give you Eternal Life.

**THERE IS NO LIFE EXCEPT THE LIFE
GIVEN BY CHRIST JESUS,
ANYTHING LESS IS EXISTING,
NOT LIFE.**

Chapter 4

The Truth of the Bible
Is beyond compare.

GOD is trustworthy; you can depend on his word.
The answer to "Can you give me any facts that would make me believe the Bible?" is yes I can, both in historical and spiritual facts. Without delving into all the implications of prophesies and all the historical facts, here are some quick answers, that are proof on their face or title, all of which can be proven in historical records and scientific proofs? Every new discovery confirms the bible; the Dead Sea Scrolls, the Rosetta stone, DNA, archeological proofs and scientific proofs.

The Bibles bought in 2013 in America
    There are 50 Bibles bought every minute, 3,000 each hour, 72,000 each day, 26.6 million in the year. Since Bible records have been kept at the American Bible Association approximately 7,000,000,000 (billion) Bibles have been added to the world; bought or given. If the Bible did not have the words of life it would not sell in these numbers.

The Old Testament
    Gives us scientific information that man did not discover for thousands of years. The Bible tells us that the earth is not flat and is spinning on an axis, also that the moon is a reflecting body and is not itself a light and more.

The Jewish People
    The oldest people recorded Biblically and in History. Just being a people with bloodlines running 6,000 years is a miracle.

Neither Egyptians nor the Chinese can prove civilization prior to 6000 years.

The Nation of Israel

The oldest continuing Nation returned to its land, in one day, as prophesied in Isaiah Continuing after hundreds of attempts to annihilate the Jewish People.

The Hebrew Language

The beginning of all languages known, recorded, and still spoken. And Hebrew is probably the language spoken by Adam when created as a full grown man. The first Book (or one of the earliest) and first usable written language.

GOD wrote the Ten Commandments in a language on two tablets that are recorded in History by secular writers in books other than the bible and the tablets were kept in the Ark of the Covenant. And the people had to have a written language to understand GOD's writing.

The incredible food and fruit production from the Israeli desert started after 1948.

The transformation of a barren wilderness in 1948, which now blooms as prophesied.

Proof of Noah's Flood

Scientists can now show evidence of the flood on each continent.

Abraham, the Patriarch of three religions.

As GOD spoke to Abraham, you will be the Father of many nations.

Prophecies of Jesus are all confirmed.

There are over 300 fulfilled prophesies of Jesus Christ's first coming. No Prophesies of Jesus, first coming, not confirmed.
There are no prophesies left unfulfilled announcing Jesus Christ first coming.

The discovery of the ancient city of Nineveh.
More evidence of a Biblical event proven.

The discovery of the cities of Sodom and Gomorrah and the brimstone that burned them up.
More evidence of a Biblical event confirmed including the cause of the destruction.

The historical fact, Jericho, a biblical city is the oldest city in the world.
The extra biblical writings about Jesus including His Resurrection recorded in many historical writings.

Can anyone argue with these facts, can anyone come up with a plausible explanation for these events and prophesies, is there any other records of any societies, Nations, or GOD to compare? Is there another book on Earth with any provable prophesies from thousands of years ago.

Why is the Bible
So important to successful living and
The lack of a Bible based society so plagued with destruction?

Absent, laws based on a loving GOD and respect for created life, is a world in which the only law in place is the "law of self-preservation". The Bible commands us in excess of 200 times to "Fear not", this WARNING by GOD on so many occasions, indicates the importance of a support system to deal with fear. Freedom and self-sufficiency is not resident in a baby, but must be taught and can only be taught in a society that believes in a Creator GOD. Freedom will not be taught in a society based on fear and self-preservation and subject to the strongest and meanest because freedom does not further the goals of despots.

Freedom must be taught. After 430 years, Israel left the slavery of Egypt and started toward the Promised Land. GOD started teaching the Jews how to be free, on the way to Canaan, GOD started training leaders, GOD gave the laws; dietary for health, social for family order, worship for respecting their Creator, government for tribal cohesiveness, and general laws for the nation for order. Functioning Societies don't just happen. All successful societies have covenants with each other to protect the rights of people, property, and freedoms. The concept of "respect for your neighbor or brother" only happens in societies that love and respect GOD.

President Obama, signed an initiative called, "My Brother's Keeper" launching an attempt to help young men of color get out of poverty, stay out of crime, and offer support for being raised in a home without a father. The problem not being addressed is the systematic elimination of GOD from schools curriculums, the acceptance of sex without marriage, and families without fathers; has produced an underclass of children who know no hope, who if they don't turn to GOD will turn to fear and self-preservation leading to jail for the majority. It is just like the government, who did not fight to keep our Christian heritage in schools, to name a program from the Bible and choose an inappropriate scripture." Am I my brother's keeper?" is Cain's answer to GOD when GOD asked Cain where was Abel, his brother, God knowing that Cain had murdered Abel. The Golden rule of "Do unto others as you would have them do to you" is probably the concept President Obama was trying to communicate or "Love your GOD with all your heart and your brother as yourself". "My Brother's Keeper" program is always going to fail because money will not replace the need for GOD and a father in the life of a young man or woman.

With GOD it's not **"my way or the highway"** With GOD it is, **"His way is the Freeway"**. For those that love The Lord, we have the benefits of the history of GOD and all His miracles: the parting of the Red Sea, Noah's Flood and the rainbow, the pillar of cloud by day and the pillar of fire by night, the virgin birth, the Resurrection, and more. Man is the only creation on earth that can worship and praise GOD and was designed to receive communication from GOD; It is an awesome privilege for believers to know that GOD exists and that He loves his creation and we don't have to fear today or tomorrow. Without GOD you do not have any mechanisms available to divert fear from overwhelming your existence. Fear, causing strife, is the opposite of faith for the hope that will give you rest and peace.

In our school systems, the knowledge of GOD is being withheld from those that need it, because of political correctness. Atheists, secularists, and anti-GOD supporters are perverting laws designed to protect worship of GOD Almighty and to follow a moral code based on loving you neighbor as yourself. One terrible result of the move of society away from GOD is a sexually active single parent family that is causing the education system, the law enforcement system, the social welfare system to be overwhelmed with clients that are dependent on the government and have matured without GOD, hope, or purpose. Fortunately for the World, GOD, Himself has declared that in the last days He will pour out HIS Spirit out on all flesh. There will be a choice for every individual to receive Jesus Christ as your savior or choose death.

Eternity does not start when you die, but when you are born again. Remember you are a "Spiritual being" having a human experience.

For **GOD**
so loved the world,
that he gave his only begotten son,
that whosoever believeth in HIM,
should not perish, but
have (echo) everlasting life. (Greek work echo meaning now)
John 3:16
The promise is for today, the **tense of the verb "have". "Have" is in the present tense** and connects believers to Eternity "now", this re-ordering of our life, and should build our faith to bring the earthly natural life (seen world) and eternal life (unseen world) together. If we have "Eternal Life" now, then our new life is where GOD is, in His omnipresence. In most conversions to Christianity we find our need for a savior for our sin debt, but we don't always continue to grow in the knowledge of God to understand the love and grandeur of our GOD and the incredible benefits of a re-ordered life. After Salvation the most important thing we can do is seek first the Kingdom of GOD and His righteousness, and endeavor to stay in that special place with GOD. Our promise from Jesus, "is abide in Him and He will abide in us". There is no greater fact, than GOD **wants** to abide in us and **wants us** to abide in Him. If you have wisdom to comprehend what this means; this is larger than the atom bomb; this is the rebirth of the '"Adam" bomb, right standing with GOD. **Do not overlook the first phrase** "For GOD so loved the world", GOD's LOVE IS CONSTANT, IT IS WHO GOD IS, you can't earn it and you can't lose GOD's Love. You can refuse to look at it, refuse to receive it, refuse to live in it, refuse to benefit from it, but you can't change it because GOD is Love. It is part of GOD's perfectness. As a parent, there is nothing that I have, that I would not give to my

child and Father GOD will not withhold anything you ask that is in his will for you.

Eye hath not seen, nor ear heard,
neither have entered into the heart of man,
the things which God hath prepared for them that love him.
1 Cor 2:9

Let these promises revolutionize your life.

We have been invited to be the bride at the "Marriage supper of the Lamb",

> Rev 19:7 Let us be glad and rejoice and give Him glory, for the marriage of the Lamb has come, and His wife has made herself ready." And to her it was granted to be arrayed in fine linen, clean and bright, for the fine linen is the righteous acts of the saints. Then he said to me, "Write: 'Blessed are those who are called to the marriage supper of the Lamb!'" And he said to me, "These are the true sayings of God."

The church is the bridegroom for the Head of the church,
We are the Bride of Christ,

> Rev_21:2 Then I, John, saw the holy city, New Jerusalem, coming down out of heaven from God, prepared as a bride adorned for her husband. 21:9 Then one of the seven angels who had the seven bowls filled with the seven last plagues came to me and talked with me, saying, "Come, I will show you the bride, the Lamb's wife." 22:17 And the Spirit and the bride say, "Come!" And let him who hears say, "Come!" And let him who thirsts come. Whoever desires, let him take the water of life freely.

We are Heirs and Joint heirs with Jesus Christ to the Kingdom,

Rom_8:17 and if children, then heirs—heirs of God and joint heirs with Christ, if indeed we suffer with Him, that we may also be glorified together.

Gal_3:29 and if you are Christ's, then you are Abraham's seed, and heirs according to the promise.

Eph_3:6 that the Gentiles should be fellow heirs, of the same body, and partakers of His promise in Christ through the gospel,

Tit_3:7 that having been justified by His grace we should become heirs according to the hope of eternal life.

Heb_6:17 Thus God, determining to show more abundantly to the heirs of promise the immutability of His counsel, confirmed it by an oath,

Heb_11:9 By faith he dwelt in the land of promise as in a foreign country, dwelling in tents with Isaac and Jacob, the heirs with him of the same promise; and heirs of the kingdom which He promised to those who love Him?

Rom_4:14 For if those who are of the law are heirs, faith is made void and the promise made of no effect,

We have been made Kings and Priests,

Rev_1:6 and has made us kings and priests to His God and Father, to Him be glory and dominion forever and ever. Amen.

Rev_5:10 and have made us kings and priests to our God; And we shall reign on the earth."

Jesus has gone to prepare a new world for us,

John_14:2 In My Father's house are many mansions; if it were not so, I would have told you. I go to prepare a place for you.

John_14:3 And if I go and prepare a place for you, I will come again and receive you to Myself; that where I am, there you may be also.

We will join Him and have an everlasting life.

> Dan_12:2 And many of those who sleep in the dust of the earth shall awake, Some to everlasting life, Some to shame and everlasting contempt.
>
> John_3:16 For God so loved the world that He gave His only begotten Son, that whoever believes in Him should not perish but have everlasting life.
>
> John_3:36 He who believes in the Son has everlasting life; and he who does not believe the Son shall not see life, but the wrath of God abides on him."
>
> John_4:14 but whoever drinks of the water that I shall give him will never thirst. But the water that I shall give him will become in him a fountain of water springing up into everlasting life."
>
> John_5:24 "Most assuredly, I say to you, he who hears My word and believes in Him who sent Me, has everlasting life, and shall not come into judgment, but has passed from death into life.
>
> John_6:27 Do not labor for the food which perishes, but for the food which endures to everlasting life, which the Son of Man will give you, because God the Father has set His seal on Him."
>
> John_6:40 And this is the will of Him who sent Me, that everyone who sees the Son and believes in Him may have everlasting life; and I will raise him up at the last day."
>
> John_6:47 Most assuredly, I say to you, he who believes in Me has everlasting life.
>
> John 12:49 For I have not spoken on My own authority; but the Father who sent Me gave Me a command, what I should say and what I should speak. And I know that His command is everlasting life. Therefore, whatever I speak, just as the Father has told Me, so I speak."

Act_13:46 Then Paul and Barnabas grew bold and said, "It was necessary that the word of God should be spoken to you first; but since you reject it, and judge yourselves unworthy of everlasting life, behold, we turn to the Gentiles.

Rom_6:22 But now having been set free from sin, and having become slaves of God, you have your fruit to holiness, and the end, everlasting life.

Gal_6:8 for he who sows to his flesh will of the flesh reap corruption, but he who sows to the Spirit will of the Spirit reap everlasting life.

1Ti_1:16 However, for this reason I obtained mercy, that in me first Jesus Christ might show all longsuffering, as a pattern to those who are going to believe on Him for everlasting life.

**The Bible is the only book that contains the "Words of Life",
the beauty of this world glorifies its creator,
mankind was formed in the image of GOD,
the heavens are alive with GOD's glory,
and because of GOD's love there is hope,
through the grace offered by Jesus Christ.**

Man does not live by Bread alone but by every word that proceedeth out of the mouth of GOD. (Matthew 4:4)

In natural terms, we hear this verse and think about foods we eat, but God is saying that **you cannot live without the "Word of GOD", you can only exist.** Life is more than food and drink. Providing our daily physical needs may be what we concentrate our efforts to achieve but there can't be life without God. There is only existence without purpose.

The names of Jesus

Transform existing to Eternal living
By controlling the seen world with the power of the unseen.

Why are there so many names for GOD and Jesus Christ?
Everything about the Names of Jesus and the references to the Lord's existence as the natural elements of our life, like water, bread, etc. tell us about how much our GOD cares about our well being. The following scriptures are examples of Names or references that speak to our Eternal life through our existence on earth. Life unspeakable in Jesus on Earth and Eternity.

Jesus is the spring of living water
> John_4:10 Jesus answered and said to her, "If you knew the gift of God, and who it is who says to you, 'Give Me a drink,' you would have asked Him, and He would have given you living water." The woman said to Him, "Sir, You have nothing to draw with, and the well is deep. Where then do You get that living water? He who believes in Me, as the Scripture has said, out of his heart will flow rivers of living water."

Jesus is the light to the world and the light of life.
> John_8:12 Then Jesus spoke to them again, saying, "I am the light of the world. He who follows Me shall not walk in darkness, but have the light of life."
> John_9:5 As long as I am in the world, I am the light of the world."
> 1Th 5:5 Ye are all the children of light, and the children of the day: we are not of the night, nor of darkness.

Jesus is the bread of life
> John_6:33 For the bread of God is He who comes down from heaven and gives life to the world."

John_6:35 And Jesus said to them, "I am the bread of life. He who comes to Me shall never hunger, and he who believes in Me shall never thirst.

John_6:48 I am the bread of life.

John_6:51 I am the living bread which came down from heaven. If anyone eats of this bread, he will live forever; and the bread that I shall give is My flesh, which I shall give for the life of the world."

When you hear these Names what do you think about the expressions?

Jesus is the "Bread of Life".

Jesus is the spring of "Living Water".

Jesus is the "Passover Lamb".

Jesus is the "Light of life".

Notice that, we cannot eat Jesus, we cannot drink Jesus, Jesus does not look like a lamb, Jesus does not look similar to a light, but this assimilation of Jesus with our basic needs gives us confidence, that Almighty GOD will use the power of the unseen world to control the seen world. Christ associated His life, His names, and His power to identify with aspects of our daily life. The names of our Savior speak to the confidence we can have over every part of our natural life. Jesus cares and described himself in terms that answer each need in our life.

Seek ye first the Kingdom of GOD and His righteousness and all these (natural) things shall be added unto you;

Jesus is the fountain of living waters

Jesus is the light of the world

Jesus is the Bread of Life

Jesus is Love

Jesus is the Word

Jesus is first born from the dead

Jesus is coming again that we might be where He is

Jesus is our High Priest
Jesus invites us to enter his rest and more.

Jesus has given his heirs, the name above every name named, the Name of Jesus. To explain further if you were playing Rock, Paper, Scissors, Jesus; the name Jesus would win every game. Our Brother, Savior, High Priest and GOD, has been given a name, **that is above every name named** and His name has been given to us. His name is above the name of wealth, health, anger, headaches, cancer, fear, and any other name you can name.

You must take your eyes off this world
So that you can see who you are in the Spiritual World.

The Believers verse of victory. Jesus has already given you what you need. Be enlightened.
> That the God of our Lord Jesus Christ, the Father of glory, will give (didomi) unto you the spirit of wisdom and revelation in the knowledge of him:
> The eyes of your understanding being enlightened;
> that ye have (eido) what is the hope of his calling, and what the riches of the glory of his inheritance in the saints, And what is the exceeding greatness of his power to us-ward who believe, according to the working of his mighty power, Which he wrought in Christ, when he raised him from the dead, and set him at his own right hand in the heavenly places, Far above all principality, and power, and might, and dominion, **and every name that is named**, not only in this world, but also in that which is to come: Ephesians 1:17-21

When Paul describes the riches of our inheritance in Christ for believers, **his inheritance to us is now** and in the future, "this world and the world to come".

Names of God and Jesus Christ are perfect in their description and they are Truth. Here is a list of one hundred references to the Name of Jesus that identify who He is and what he is to our natural and spiritual lives. Jesus has experienced any temptation we have experienced and has given his names for us to call on in any situation we find ourselves.

Aleph and Tav (GOD) Gen 1:1 Rev. 1:8 Matt 28:18, Advocate (1 John 2:1) Almighty (Rev. 1:8; 22:13) Amen (Rev. 3:14) Apostle of our Profession (Heb. 3:1) Atoning Sacrifice for our Sins (1 John 2:2) Author of Life (Acts 3:15) Author and Perfecter of our Faith (Heb. 12:2) Author of Salvation (Heb. 2:10) Beginning and End (Rev. 22:13) Blessed and only Ruler (1 Tim. 6:15) Bread of God (John 6:33) Bread of Life (John 6:35; 6:48) Capstone (Acts 4:11; 1 Pet. 2:7) Chief Cornerstone (Eph. 2:20) Chief Shepherd (1 Pet. 5:4) Christ (1 John 2:22) Creator (John 1:3) Deliverer (Rom. 11:26) Eternal Life (1 John 1:2; 5:20) Everlasting Father (Isa. 9:6) Gate (John 10:9) Faithful and True (Rev. 19:11) Faithful Witness (Rev. 1:5) Faith and True Witness (Rev. 3:14) First and Last (Rev. 1:17; 2:8; 22:13) Firstborn From the Dead (Rev. 1:5) Good Shepherd (John 10:11,14) Great Shepherd (Heb. 13:20) Great High Priest (Heb. 4:14) Head of the Church (Eph. 1:22; 4:15; 5:23) Heir of all things (Heb. 1:2) High Priest (Heb. 2:17) Holy and True (Rev. 3:7) Holy One (Acts 3:14) Hope (1 Tim. 1:1) Hope of Glory (Col. 1:27) Horn of Salvation (Luke 1:69) I Am (John 8:58) Image of God (2 Cor. 4:4) King Eternal (1 Tim. 1:17) King of Israel (John 1:49) King of the Jews (Mt. 27:11) King of kings (1 Tim 6:15; Rev. 19:16) King of the Ages (Rev. 15:3) Lamb (Rev. 13:8) Lamb of God (John 1:29) Lamb Without Blemish (1 Pet. 1:19) Last Adam (1 Cor. 15:45) Life (John 14:6; Col. 3:4) Light of the World (John 8:12) Lion of the Tribe of Judah (Rev. 5:5) Living One (Rev. 1:18) Living Stone (1 Pet. 2:4) Lord (2 Pet. 2:20) Lord of All (Acts 10:36) Lord of Glory (1 Cor. 2:8) Lord of lords

(Rev. 19:16) LORD [YHWH] our Righteousness (Jer. 23:6) Man from Heaven (1 Cor. 15:48) Mediator of the New Covenant (Heb. 9:15) Mighty God (Isa. 9:6) Morning Star (Rev. 22:16) Offspring of David (Rev. 22:16) Only Begotten Son of God (John 1:18; 1 John 4:9) Our Great God and Savior (Titus 2:13) Our Holiness (1 Cor. 1:30) Our Husband (2 Cor. 11:2) Our Protection (2 Thess. 3:3) Our Righteousness (1 Cor. 1:30) Our Sacrificed Passover Lamb (1 Cor. 5:7) Power of God (1 Cor. 1:24) Precious Cornerstone (1 Pet. 2:6) Prince of Peace (Isa. 9:6) Prophet (Acts 3:22) Resurrection and Life (John 11:25) Righteous Branch (Jer. 23:5) Righteous One (Acts 7:52; 1 John 2:1) Rock (1 Cor. 10:4) Root of David (Rev. 5:5; 22:16) Ruler of God's Creation (Rev. 3:14) Ruler of the Kings of the Earth (Rev. 1:5) Savior (Eph. 5:23; Titus 1:4; 3:6; 2 Pet. 2:20)   Son of David (Lk. 18:39) Son of God (John 1:49; Heb. 4:14) Son of Man (Mt. 8:20) Son of the Most High God (Lk. 1:32) Source of Eternal Salvation for all who obey him (Heb. 5:9) The One Mediator (1 Tim. 2:5) The Stone the builders rejected (Acts 4:11) True Bread (John 6:32) True Light (John 1:9) True Vine (John 15:1) Truth (John 1:14; 14:6) Way (John 14:6) Wisdom of God (1 Cor. 1:24) Wonderful Counselor (Isa. 9:6) Word (John 1:1) Word of God (Rev. 19:13)

Throughout the entire Creation story when GOD gives something a name, inherent in the name is the completion of its purpose. GOD changed the name of Abram which means "High Father", to Abraham which means "Father of a Multitude or Father of many nations". GOD did this by adding the fifth letter of the Hebrew alphabet to Abram. The fifth letter is hei and is the figure for "Grace" and appears twice in GOD's Hebrew name Yahweh. (Yud Hei Vav Hei) Abraham's wife Sarai which means "My princess" is changed to Sarah which means "Mother of Nations" Hei the Hebrew figure for Grace and part of GOD's Holiest name was added to Sarah's name. GOD, when naming people gave them a name that would accomplish the goal inherent in their name.

Jesus gave believers the name "Salt of the Earth", we are here to flavor a world in sin.

We have been dropped in the stream of life by GOD to give the world flavor by being a child of the King and the "Salt of the Earth". Our responsibility to a loving GOD is to bring the aspects of a loving Creator God to the earth. There is no Love for your neighbor in a world without GOD, because there is no love without GOD, but by acts of kindness and a life of submission to GOD, we can change the world one good deed at a time and one repentant sinner at a time.

Jesus called believers the "salt of the earth". Let us explore some of the references for salt in the bible and the importance of salt to us. We can enhance the flavor of the world with the love of GOD given to us. Jesus, in the greatest sermon ever preached, "The Sermon on the Mount"

> Mat 5:13 Ye are the salt of the earth: but if the salt have lost his savour, wherewith shall it be salted? It is thenceforth good for nothing, but to be cast out, and to be trodden under foot of men.

We must allow everyone to know that we are a child of the King and we matter and we would like everyone to know King Jesus as we know the King and submit and have Everlasting life.

Elisha, the great Prophet, faced a serious problem when the spring serving the city became poisoned and was causing the land to go barren and people to be poisoned.

> The men of the city said to Elisha, "My lord can see that this is a pleasant city to live in; but the water is bad, so that the ground is causing miscarriages." "Bring me a new jug," he said, "and put salt in it." They brought it to him. He went out

to the source of the water, threw salt into it and said, "This is what Adonai says: 'I have healed this water; it will no longer cause death or miscarrying.' " The water was healed and has remained healed to this day, in keeping with Elisha's spoken word. 2 Kings 2:19-21

Salt was added to sacrifices in the temple to create even greater savory incense to the offering to the LORD.

Lev 2:13 And every oblation of thy meat offering shalt thou season with salt; neither shalt thou suffer the salt of the covenant of thy God to be lacking from thy meat offering: with all thine offerings thou shalt offer salt.

Num 18:19 All the heave (wave) offerings of the holy things, which the children of Israel offer unto the LORD, have I given thee, and thy sons and thy daughters with thee, by a statute forever: it is a covenant of salt for ever before the LORD unto thee and to thy seed with thee.

We are part of the guarantee, that the Salt covenant, given to David's line of descendants would be everlasting kings.

2Ch 13:5 Ought ye not to know that the LORD God of Israel gave the kingdom over Israel to David forever, even to him and to his sons by a covenant of salt?'

The Kingly line of David and all Believers are part of the salt covenant and Jesus is our King of Kings.

WE ARE THE KINGS IN "KING OF KINGS"
AND WE ARE THE PRIESTS
FOR WHOM JESUS IS THE HIGH PRIEST.
WE ARE THE LORDS IN "LORD OF LORDS"

Notes

Chapter 5

Your eye will only see
what your mind is ready to comprehend

In your heart, do you believe GOD created the Cosmos, the Heavens and the Earth, seed bearing plants, Mankind, and all the creatures on the land and seas? More important, can your mind's eye comprehend GOD's love for you and HIS gift of HIS SON, to be sacrificed for your sins and give to you Eternal life through belief in Jesus Christ. We must develop a view of GOD that beholds the magnitude of his being. **Everything about GOD is absolute and works to perfection and is beautiful in Holiness** (Holiness which means separate or set apart because of its perfectness).

FACT: The gift of Righteousness that we have been given is greater than the entire body of sin in the world from the beginning of time until forever.

Let us start with this description of God and then let the Holy Spirit show us more.

GOD is holy and beautiful in His omniscience, since no one but GOD knows all things.

His omnipresence and omnipotence are also utterly unique and, without flaw.

In all of His attributes In His freedom, eternality, self-existence, love, justice, mercy, grace, forgiveness, and truth, GOD is absolute, holy, and magnificent. Since His attributes are perfection, they are set apart from any aspect of failure! God's holiness and, therefore, His beauty extend to every aspect of His being. Therefore, GOD is gloriously and overwhelmingly beautiful in His perfection.

When we understand the incomprehensible grandeur of our GOD, Then we may realize the Love GOD has for mankind and our incredible worth to GOD.

**One obstacle keeping us from
The power of GOD is
Our view of GOD falls so short of the reality of God.**

Jesus did not come to make bad men good. **He came to make dead men alive.** It is this fact; that makes it so important to be motivated by your position in Christ and not motivated by fear of failing in your performance as a Christian. The Torah or the law demanded actions (sacrifices for sin) from mankind, but the Grace of Jesus Christ came to provide (salvation) for us.

"Jesus said I have come to serve and save that which was lost."

And "I am come that you might have life and have it more abundantly". John 10:10

The Life Jesus came to bring us, is not of this world because it is eternal and our Spirit was activated at Salvation, not our death.

The historic aspects of the Torah resulted in lives being consumed with a "conscience of sin" and sacrifices for every sin or bad deed. GOD's new Covenant wants us to live concentrating on the "perfect" righteousness of Jesus Christ. GOD promises, in the new covenant written on our hearts, that HE will remember our sins no more. **GOD condemned the "Sin in the flesh" and satisfied His righteous judgment for sin by the execution of a sinless man** (Romans 8:3). To say it in another way, the new life in Jesus is not about living right, it is about believing right. Grace is not a license to live recklessly, but instead grace is receiving GOD's love and allowing that love to motivate right living in a Spiritual life on Earth and after in Heaven.

The Cross of Jesus Christ was visible by the people in Jerusalem 1986 years ago but more important to us today, the Cross of Jesus is outside time, it is in the Eternal Spirit realm where there is no time. The Spirit realm is something believers can and should live in every day but not every believer appropriates its power and uses the unseen spiritual world to control the seen world. It is this ability for the cross to take away the sins of the world; past, present, and future, that we can partake of the salvation offered at the Cross nearly 2000 years ago, but available today. It is because of the perfection of the attributes of GOD; the Sacrificial Punishment was perfect and was an overpayment for the Perfect Justice of GOD.

GOD condemned the "sin in the flesh", or in other words, GOD executed the punishment against sin in Human nature, so we could have right standing with GOD though Jesus Christ. Our "Position in Christ".

> **there is therefore now no condemnation to those who are in Christ Jesus**, who do not walk according to the flesh, but according to the Spirit. For the law of the Spirit of life in Christ Jesus has made me free from the law of sin and death. For what the law could not do in that it was weak through the flesh, God did by sending His own Son in the likeness of sinful flesh, on account of sin: **He (GOD) condemned "sin in the flesh", that the righteous requirement of the law might be fulfilled in us who do not walk according to the flesh but according to the Spirit.** For those who live according to the flesh set their minds on the things of the flesh, but those who live according to the Spirit, the things of the Spirit. For to be carnally minded is death, but to be spiritually minded is life and peace. Romans 8:1

By GOD condemning the "sin in the flesh",
Sin no longer has control over believers,
Separating us from GOD.

The righteous requirement of the law has been fulfilled, now we must continue walking in the Spirit, not worrying about sin because GOD condemned "sin in the flesh" and established our "Position in Christ". Believers will want to concentrate on our "Performance after Salvation" because of its benefits when lived in the Spirit: it pleases God and it keeps the Believer in perfect peace. And God's action has re-ordered life, so that we can be assured of our "Position in Christ" and not live in fear of doing something wrong but love doing something good. When love is any part of an activity, the activity is for the benefit of another and giving of yourself for others is what life with GOD is all about.

There are many moving parts to the New Life in Jesus Christ that the Bible speaks to and we must understand;

Our Spirit is born again. Our bodies are not redeemed. Our physical lives are in a battle between living in the Spirit producing the Fruit of the Spirit, or following the desires of the physical body evidencing the works of the flesh. Our performance as a Christian, and the Temple of the Holy Spirit, can lose fellowship (communication) with GOD's power if we get caught up in the works of the flesh. Our fellowship can be restored by changing our direction back to producing the Fruit of the Spirit. Our "Position in Christ" is not lost because, **a human error cannot counter a perfect act of Salvation given by God.** After Salvation, our faith is now the evidence of our hope for our redeemed bodies at the resurrection and the second coming of Jesus Christ.

> Faith is the substance of things hoped for the evidence of things not seen.

After salvation, the next thing we hope for is the redemption of our bodies and the second coming of Jesus Christ which happen at the same time. Think about the scripture from Hebrews 11:1 Hope is first or primary subject of this sentence, so that faith can give it substance. Paul in Romans explains the next hope for believers.

> … we ourselves, who have the first fruits of the Spirit, groan inwardly as we continue waiting eagerly to be made sons — that is, to have our whole bodies redeemed and set free. It was in this hope that we were saved. But if we see what we hope for, it isn't hope — after all, who hopes for what he already sees? But if we continue hoping for something we don't see, then we still wait eagerly for it, with perseverance. Romans 8:23-25

Consider Jesus words at the washing of the disciples feet, Peter asked the Lord to bathe him all over but GOD said Peter,

> **"If you have been bathed you are clean and only need your feet cleaned. And all of you are clean save one (Judas)".**

Jesus is showing us the way to stay forgiven so that we can stay in fellowship with Almighty GOD. <u>Believers have been bathed in the Blood of Jesus and are clean and when we fall into works of the flesh we need our feet washed.</u> Fortunately we have an Advocate with God so that when we ask for forgiveness for our performance, Jesus, our Advocate with the Father, is faithful to forgive us.

> "if any man sin, we have an advocate with the Father, Jesus Christ the righteous" (1 John 2:1).

When you love GOD and you miss the mark with your performance it will hurt your heart that you missed doing the will of God, and did something you chose to do, knowing it was wrong.

GOD says to purge our Conscience, It appears, that man received a conscience when Adam sinned and received the knowledge of Good and evil and became subject to time.

The reasons for this belief are:
      Adam and Eve realized they were naked.
      Adam and Eve hid with shame.
      Adam and Eve covered their reproductive parts with leaves.
      Adam blamed the woman, Eve blamed the Devil.
      Adam blamed GOD for giving him the woman.

None of these feelings were part of their make up until they had knowledge of Good and evil. The fruit of a conscience is fear and fear is not compatible with faith. Adam and Eve chose Satan's lie over GOD's truth that if they ate of the forbidden tree, it would produce death. They re-ordered life, AS THEY KNEW IT, with their choice and brought on death and the curse on all of mankind. It is now incumbent on us to make a choice that re-orders our life by choosing the sacrifice of Jesus Christ for our sins. Salvation establishes our "Position in Christ", so we can choose to concentrate on the Gift of Righteousness and not be sin conscious. God wants our motivation to live right and fellowship with Father GOD to be an act of love not fear, condemnation, or conscience.

We have freedom to exchange Sin Consciousness, for Righteousness conscious and reign in life through the one man Jesus Christ.
      For if by the one man's offense death reined through the one, much more those who receive the abundance of grace and of the gift of righteousness **will reign in life through the One, Jesus Christ.** Therefore, as through one man's offense judgment came to all men, resulting in condemnation, even so through one Man's righteous act the free gift came to all men, resulting in justification of life. Romans 5:12-18 NKJB

Instead of concentrating on not meeting the goal of righteous living, we concentrate on believing the love that GOD has for us, to change our motivation from fear of doing wrong, to loving to do right. Right believing will lead to right living. Our life is no longer dependent on what we can do, **but instead on what Jesus has already done.**

The Holy Spirit
convicts
Believers of Righteousness, not sin.

Jesus description of the Holy Spirit's benefits and power.

> John 16 The Holy spirit is sent as our comforter to convict Christians of our Righteousness, to convict the non-believers of sin, and to announce that Satan has been judged.
>
> And when He (Holy Spirit) has come, He will convict the world of sin, and of righteousness, and of judgment: Of sin, because they do not believe in Me; (notice these people are non believers) Of righteousness, because I go to My Father and you see Me no more; (Believers) Of judgment, because the ruler of this world is judged. John 16:9-10 (Satan's judgment)

Expand your view of GOD, the Holy Spirit is no longer convicting you of sin in your life. After your sins have been forgiven the Holy Spirit is reminding you of God's love for you. It is the love from GOD to you that disappoints you when you find yourself following the flesh instead of the Spirit. The Holy Spirit is inside you to tell you about the sacrifice that Jesus made for you because THE GODHEAD loves you.

For GOD
So loved the world
That HE gave HIS only Son

That whosoever believeth in Him
Should not perish but have everlasting life.

We must allow the enormity of GOD's love for mankind to change our view of ourselves. If GOD Almighty condemned sin in the flesh and gave us perfect righteousness through his Son, Jesus Christ, we must assume that position in GOD.

When Jesus said, "I am the way the truth and the life". John 14:6
>It is GOD speaking (I Am) the way, when perfected; I am all of Salvation,
>(I am) the Truth, that is the completion of all facts, and
>(I am) the source of life, both natural and Eternal.

We must believe in the gross overpayment of our sins by our Savior; it is our position in HIS Sacrifice that makes us worthy to be in right standing with GOD. Our performance will never measure up but His sacrifice has been accepted for the sin of the entire world. If you can't imagine yourself forgiven and in right standing with GOD through the death of His Dear Son, how can you imagine GOD being able to fellowship with you in your sinful state?

As Jesus is (right now), so are we (right now) in this world, therefore we are not condemned.

>And we have known and believed the love that God has for us. God is love, and he who abides in love abides in God and God in him. Love has been perfected among us in this: that we may have boldness in the Day of Judgment; because as He, Jesus Christ, is, so are we in this world. 1 John 4:16-17

If a believer is not committed to GOD, you may break your daily fellowship, but a human cannot reverse your Position in Jesus Christ which God has finished.

It is easy to want GOD's attributes to beat down your enemy but that is not what GOD is about. You can't use GOD and you don't need to try to manipulate GOD but instead love GOD with all your heart and you will find a loving Father. And a loving Father would not withhold anything he could give to his children for their benefit. If your relationship with GOD is from a Spirit of Love and free will, then nothing will be withheld from you. Remember the Lords Prayer "thy kingdom come, thy will be done on Earth as it is in Heaven"

> "If you abide in me and
> my words abide in you
> ask what you will and it will be done for you" John 15:7

Notice the choices we make affect our prayer life; "If you abide in me and my words abide in you" is a condition for our prayers to be granted. When someone in your family moves to another country you lose fellowship with that person, but you do not lose relationship. A similar thing happens when you're a child of GOD. You have a relationship with God and the Holy Spirit comes to abide in you as a seal to the covenant of your relationship with Jesus Christ. If works of the flesh regain a foothold in your life you will lose fellowship with the Holy Spirit and you might think that the heavens are brass and your prayers are not getting through but the truth is that you haven't lost relationship, you have lost fellowship. After salvation you are judged on your faithfulness not sinfulness. The Holy Spirit will convict you of your righteousness in Jesus Christ and you will have a choice to re-enter GOD's rest and peace. You have to find the break in your fellowship with the Holy Spirit. Generally the word of GOD is not abiding in you. Fortunately your advocate with The

Father loves you and will restore fellowship. Filling your heart with the word of GOD will increase the peace in your heart and take away barriers to your prayer life.

At the "Believers" Judgment, before Jesus Christ, we are going to give account of our lives both good and bad and our deeds will be proven by fire and we will receive a reward for the deeds that produced fruit of the Spirit and we will suffer loss for the deeds of the flesh. Romans 14:10-12 II Corinthians 5:10

> 2Co 5:10 For we must all appear before the judgment seat of Christ; that every one may receive the things done in his body, according to that he hath done, whether it be good or bad.

A reminder, it is at the "Believers" judgment, which mean after your salvation, you are a believer and Heaven is assured. The question is what rewards and crowns will you be given to present to GOD when you see HIM? (II Timothy 2:5 and 4:8, James 1:12, I Peter 5:4, Revelation 2:10, and James 1:12)

Chapter 6

Overcome evil with good.

For those that, by choice, love themselves and don't recognize "The Creator", they are doomed to live without the power of the "The Creator" on their behalf, and their sensual pleasure is "As good as it gets". Their pleasure is their only reward and it won't make them want to be a better person.

When "by choice", people don't recognize the Creator, GOD, there is no authority to answer for their thoughts or actions. These people suppress their conscience and believe they know what is best for their existence. Without an authority to answer for your actions, nothing is wrong with your thoughts or your deeds. These people don't believe in GOD and have not thought of the future because they don't know if there will be another tomorrow. **They replace GOD with themselves.**

If you are a believer in GOD and Jesus Christ, you do not have a conscience as a burden but as a gift. Our conscience allows our thoughts and actions to be brought before our heart so that we can embrace them or reject them.

> Hebrews 9:14 tells us through the power of our Lords sacrifice we are to purge our conscience from dead works. Remember Romans 8:1 There is now no condemnation to those who walk not after the flesh but after the Spirit.

Listen to this variety of Biblical Authors on the Subject; godlessness. A world of Self preservation.

If there is no Hell then Heaven is not a prize.

For if **God did not spare the angels who sinned**, but cast them down to hell and delivered them into chains of darkness, to be reserved for judgment; and did not spare the ancient world, but saved Noah, one of eight people, a preacher of righteousness, bringing in the flood on the world of the ungodly 2 Peter 2:4-5; and (and in the time of Abraham) turning the cities of Sodom and Gomorrah into ashes, condemned them to destruction, making them an example to those who afterward would live ungodly; …—then the Lord knows how to deliver the godly out of temptations and to **reserve the unjust under punishment for the day of judgment**, and especially those who walk according to the flesh in the lust of uncleanness and despise authority. They are presumptuous, self-willed. They are not afraid to speak evil of dignitaries, whereas angels, who are greater in power and might, do not bring a reviling accusation against them before the Lord. But these, like natural brute beasts made to be caught and destroyed, speak evil of the things they do not understand, and will utterly perish in their own corruption, and will receive the wages of unrighteousness, as those who count it pleasure to carouse in the daytime. They are spots and blemishes, carousing in their own deceptions while they feast with you, having eyes full of adultery and that cannot cease from sin, enticing unstable souls. They have a heart trained in covetous practices, and are accursed children. They have forsaken the right way and gone astray, following the way of Balaam the son of Beor,

The New Testament scriptures speaking to a society without GOD

2Ti 3:2 People will be self-loving, money-loving, proud, arrogant, insulting, disobedient to parents, ungrateful, unholy, heartless, unappeasable, slanderous, uncontrolled, brutal, hateful of good, traitorous, headstrong, swollen with conceit, loving pleasure rather than God, as they retain the outer form of religion but deny its power.

Notice; Jealousy, greed and profit to serve themselves.

Jude 1:11 Woe to them! For they have gone in the way of Cain, have run greedily in the error of Balaam for profit, and perished in the rebellion of Korah. These are spots in your love feasts, while they feast with you without fear, serving only themselves. They are clouds without water, carried about by the winds; late autumn trees without fruit, twice dead, pulled up by the roots; raging waves of the sea, foaming up their own shame; wandering stars for whom is reserved the blackness of darkness forever.

If you love only what you see and don't believe in a Creator, your love will be consumed by fire at the Judgment.

1John 2:14 I have written to you, fathers, because **you have known Him who is from the beginning**. I have written to you, young men, because you are strong, and the word of God abides in you, and you have overcome the wicked one. Do not love the world or the things in the world. If anyone loves the world, the love of the Father is not in him. For all that is in the world—the lust of the flesh, the lust of the eyes, and the pride of life—is not of the Father but is of the world. And the world is passing away, and the lust of it; but he who does the will of God abides forever.

Beware of teachers and prophets who undermine the Truth, they are bags of wind.

2Peter 2:1 But there were also false prophets among the people, even as there will be false teachers among you, who will secretly bring in destructive heresies, even denying the

Lord who bought them, and bring on themselves swift destruction. And many will follow their destructive ways, because of whom the way of truth will be blasphemed. By covetousness they will exploit you with deceptive words; for a long time their judgment has not been idle, and their destruction does not slumber.

The man who has a talking Donkey

Who loved the wages of unrighteousness; but he was rebuked for his iniquity by a dumb donkey; clouds carried by a tempest, for who is reserved the blackness of darkness forever. For when they speak great swelling words of emptiness, they allure through the lusts of the flesh, through lewdness, the ones who have actually escaped from those who live in error. While they promise them liberty, they themselves are slaves of corruption; for by whom a person is overcome, by him also he is brought into bondage. For if, after they have escaped the pollutions of the world through the knowledge of the Lord and Savior Jesus Christ, they are again entangled in them and overcome, the latter end is worse for them than the beginning. For it would have been better for them not to have known the way of righteousness, than having known it, to turn from the holy commandment delivered to them.

2Pe 2:22 But it has happened to them according to the true proverb: "A DOG RETURNS TO HIS OWN VOMIT," and, "a sow, having washed, to her wallowing in the mire."

When Christians think or talk of Hell, we are adamant about not going to Hell because GOD is not there, but the Non believer is adamant about not wanting to go to Heaven because GOD is there. **GOD will not send you to a Heaven against your will and you will be allowed to have what you want.**

Eternal Life Begins at Salvation, 94

Darkness embodies aspects of existing that are evil.
We are commanded to
> **"have no fellowship with the unfruitful works of darkness,**
> but rather reprove them. For it is a shame even to speak of
> those things which are done of them in secret" (Ephesians
> 5:11-12).

Things done in secret are not done in Truth and GOD is Truth. Truth
is more than the opposite of a lie, TRUTH is the exactness of GOD's
word and the operation of the world according to what GOD spoke
and put into action. Every atom, molecule, DNA, and every other
building block GOD set in motion to operate the world is operated in
Truth.

The evil events of the night terminated at what the Bible calls "the
dawning of the day." But the Hebrew word used for "dawning"
(panah) is not the normal word for the dawn. Instead it is the word
for "turning." Thus, it is not referring to the rising of the sun, but to
the rotation of the earth which, after a dark night of evil, once again
turns its face to the "light of the world." GOD set the earth in its
rotation and made the light to bring life.

In Heaven,
not only is there no night,
there is no darkness.

For emphasis in the description of Heaven,
> "there shall be no night there" (Revelation 21:22). I saw no
> Temple in the city, for Adonai, God of heaven's armies, is its
> Temple, as is the Lamb. **The city has no need for the sun or**
> **the moon to shine on it, because God's Glory (Sh'khinah)**
> **gives it light, and its lamp is the Lamb.** The nations will
> walk by its light, and the kings of the earth will bring their

splendor into it. Its gates will never close, they stay open all day because night will not exist there, and the honor and splendor of the nations will be brought into it. Nothing impure may enter it, nor anyone who does shameful things or lies; the only ones who may enter are those whose names are written in the Lamb's Book of Life.

Rev 22:12 "And behold, I am coming quickly, and My reward is with Me, to give to every one according to his work. I am the Alpha and the Omega, the Beginning and the End, the First and the Last." Blessed are those who do His commandments that they may have the right to the tree of life, and may enter through the gates into the city. But outside are dogs and sorcerers and sexually immoral and murderers and idolaters, and whoever loves and practices a lie.
"I, Jesus, have sent My angel to testify to you these things in the churches. I am the Root and the Offspring of David, the Bright and Morning Star."

**It did not cost GOD anything
to create the sun, moons, stars, earth
and everything on earth but
it cost GOD everything to save one life.**

When Elijah called down the fire of GOD's judgment it consumed the sacrifice, the water around the altar, the stones of the altar, but when Jesus said it is finished GOD's judgment fell on Jesus and was justified. **The payment for the judgment of sin for all time was paid in Jesus Christ.**

Romans 6 GOD is not demanding of you but is your supply.

(Rom 6:13) And do not present your members as instruments of unrighteousness to sin, but present yourselves to God as being alive from the dead, and your members as instruments of righteousness to God. For sin shall not have dominion over you, **for you are not under law (demand) but under grace (supply).** What then? Shall we sin because we are not under law but under grace? Certainly not!

Do you not know that to whom you present yourselves slaves to obey, you are that one's slaves whom you obey, whether of sin leading to death, or of obedience leading to righteousness? But God be thanked that though you were slaves of sin, yet you obeyed from the heart that form of doctrine to which you were delivered. And having been set free from sin, you became slaves of righteousness.

I speak in human terms because of the weakness of your flesh. For just as you presented your members as slaves of uncleanness, and of lawlessness leading to more lawlessness, so now present your members as slaves of righteousness for holiness. For when you were slaves of sin, you were free in regard to righteousness. What fruit did you have then in the things of which you are now ashamed? For the end of those things is death. But now having been set free from sin, and having become slaves of God, you have your fruit to holiness, and the end, everlasting life. For the wages of sin is death, but the gift of God is eternal life in Christ Jesus our Lord. Also see Romans 7:1-7

Mat 22:29 Jesus answered and said to them, "You are mistaken, not knowing the Scriptures nor the power of God. For in the resurrection they neither marry nor are given in marriage, but are like angels of God in heaven. But concerning the resurrection of the dead, have you not read what was spoken to you by God, saying, 'I AM THE GOD OF ABRAHAM, THE GOD OF ISAAC, AND THE GOD OF JACOB' ? **God is not the God of the dead, but of the living."** And when the multitudes heard this, they were astonished at His teaching.

A normal activity in almost every family are the, "end of life promises"; the wills, power of attorney, and medical directives. We make these covenants with our families because we know that our bodies are mortal. When your mortality becomes evident, your desire for the unseen Spiritual world becomes paramount. At death, we need to have a "new covenant" for this new reality. Only Jesus Christ has the power to lay down his life and raise it again, but He has made that power to be resident in us. For those who "choose" to believe in Jesus Christ, as their Savior, and GOD's answer to the covenants made and, written in the Bible, can live a life with an intimate eternal relationship with GOD, available now.

Looking at our problems
Without thinking about
"How GOD looks at our problem."

Even believers, who praise GOD and love their neighbor, find themselves in situations they wish did not happen. The following section studies this situation.

The "light of life" is unseen with the eye but visible with the heart. The unseen world of GOD is the part of our lives, driven by the unseen attributes of GOD, for example: love, right standing with GOD, favor with GOD and man, faith, self-control, empathy, giving, sacrificing, and more. Even believers can find themselves, living in their "own little world": which is concentrating on the seen part of living, without the power available with GOD from the unseen world. We can be caught up looking at the problems we can see, without looking at the perceived problem as GOD sees it. GOD is interested in how you live through the perceived problem. Abiding with GOD in your daily life won't make the things we call problems go away, but it will allow you to prosper while you are experiencing what you think is a problem. A problem to us is anything that goes against what we had planned, but we may not be seeing the entire picture until we check with GOD to see what his plan was.

Take a minute, to look at Joseph's life; it consumes 25% of the book of Genesis.

1.   The perspective starts with a dream, GOD telling Joseph that, he will be a great leader and His Family will bow down to him. Joseph embraced his call from GOD and never forgot the word from GOD and trusted GOD in the midst of slavery and jail.

2.   His brothers try to kill him, but at the last minute he is sold into slavery.

3.   His new owner is Potipher, the Captain of the Guard, who makes Joseph, head of his household and Joseph prospers, while being a slave.

4.   Potipher's wife decides to seduce Joseph, but Joseph will not betray his master and his GOD. Potipher's wife accuses Joseph of rape.

5.   Potipher puts Joseph in jail for 12 years, but in a flash Joseph prospers in jail and becomes the head of the jail. While in jail Joseph interprets a dream for men who work for the Pharoh.

6.   The Pharaoh calls for Joseph to interpret his dream. After giving Pharoh GOD's interpretation of the dream Joseph is made the second in command over the Egyptian nation. Joseph tells Pharaoh that GOD has told him that the dream is of seven years of plenty and seven years of famine.

7.   During the famine, Joseph's brothers come to Egypt to buy grain because of the abundant supply and Joseph is commander in charge. His Family bows down to him and they are reunited and the rest of the family joins them and they move to the most fertile part of Egypt. Joseph was the providence of GOD sent to arrange a place for the Hebrew nation to await the next part of GOD's plan.

8.   Joseph tells the brothers, "What you meant for evil, GOD used for good."

Joseph did not get caught up in feeling sorry for himself for being sold into slavery or put in jail but kept his eye on the promise he had from GOD. Joseph prospered inside the events we consider to be dire circumstances, because he knew God was with him and he believed the dream or vision he received from GOD would come to pass. Joseph was faithful. Everything we can do to please GOD is unseen: giving, serving, loving, faithfully living, doing good, etc. are all attributes of the GOD that are within us to be used at our choice.

We are in this world but not of this world, but we are what we are in our Spirit. There will be times and situations that do not go the way we had them planned. Remember Joseph prospered in every situation he found himself involved, and was faithful to GOD and GOD was faithful to the dream He had given Joseph as a boy. GOD will be faithful to you to uphold his part of the promises he has made to all peoples, both believers and non-believers.

Also by the Author

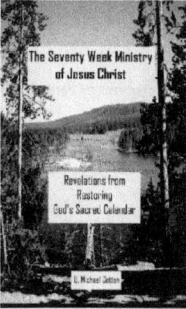

<u>The Seventy Week Ministry of Jesus Christ: Revelations from Restoring God's Sacred Calendar</u>

by Michael Cotten

ISBN: 978-0982480274

260 pages, $15.99

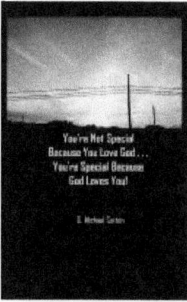

<u>You're Not Special Because You Love God . . . You're Special Because God Loves You!</u>

by Michael Cotten

ISBN: 978-1936497034

110 pages, $14.99

<u>The Passtion of the Christ: As It Really Happened</u>

by Michael Cotten

ISBN: 978-1-936497-19-5

197 pages, $16.99

9 781936 497256